More Praise for

FEAR'S EMPIRE

"In the great struggle now begun to define America's role in the post–Cold War world, Professor Barber here provides the first coherent and insightful response to the dubious and dangerous doctrines of preemptive attack and preventive war. He proposes, instead, law and contract, cooperative alliance, and expanded internationalism—all identified with the best of American diplomacy and ideals. *Fear's Empire* lays the foundation for a principled opposition based on America's truest and best values."

—Senator Gary Hart

"Although Barber is a political philosopher of the highest order, he is also an astute student of practical politics. . . . In *Fear's Empire* he brings both his theoretical and normative experience to bear, launching a scathing, yet well-balanced critique of the unilateralist posture the United States has assumed over the past three years. . . . The war on terrorism is well under way, and Barber is astute enough to realize that it must be fought."

—*San Francisco Chronicle*

"[Barber] provides a useful cautionary note for liberal empire enthusiasts."   —*Foreign Affairs*

"Barber's thesis is a tightly presented, pragmatic argument in favor of preventative democracy and multilateralism. It's embellished and made unique by its examination of the myths of moral confidence."   —*Booklist*

"A sane, brilliant and reasoned analysis of [the] darkest period in modern American history, it is essential reading for anyone wishing to understand the disaster of state terror that followed the disaster of terrorism. . . . [A] wise, erudite, succinct and wholly admirable work."   —*The Globe and Mail* (Canada)

"A sharp critique of the Bush foreign policy and strategic doctrines and of the dangerous assumptions on which they are based. This is a wise, learned and justifiably angry book, and a breath of fresh air."
—Stanley Hoffmann, Buttenwieser University Professor,
Harvard University

"Abundantly sourced and annotated. . . . Provocative work from an incisive critic who occasionally waxes unblushingly utopian."
—*Kirkus Reviews*

"Barber is not the first critic to point out the advantages of soft power as opposed to hard-handed politics. But in his perspicacity and precision he's the one who can be most dangerous to the rhetoric of Bush's neoconservative speech writers."
—*Financial Times* (Germany)

"In this dark time of hollering unreason, rampant cynicism, and preemptive war(s), *Fear's Empire* is a volume indispensable to our survival. With rare eloquence and extraordinary learning, Benjamin R. Barber marks the ever growing gap between Bush-Cheney's rule and proper democratic practice, and elucidates as well the great catastrophe that is now U.S. 'foreign policy.' The book is bracing for its clarity, humanity, large-mindedness, and common sense—and downright precious for its sound suggestions as to where we, as a nation, should be going."
—Mark Crispin Miller, author of *The Bush Dyslexicon*

FEAR'S

EMPIRE

FEAR'S

EMPIRE

War, Terrorism, and Democracy

BENJAMIN R. BARBER

W. W. Norton & Company

New York | London

For information about permission to reproduce selections from this book,
write to Permissions, W. W. Norton & Company, Inc.,
500 Fifth Avenue, New York, NY 10110

Manufacturing by Courier Westford
Book design by JAM Design
Production manager: Julia Druskin

Library of Congress Cataloging-in-Publication Data

Barber, Benjamin R., 1939–
Fear's empire : war, terrorism, and democracy /
by Benjamin R. Barber.

p. cm.
Includes bibliographical references.
ISBN 0-393-05836-0
1. United States—Foreign relations—2001– 2. United States—
Foreign relations—Philosophy. 3. United States—Military policy.
4. Intervention (International law). 5. Fear—Political aspects—United
States. 6. Terrorism—Political aspects. 7. Democracy.
8. International cooperation. 9. Globalization—Political aspects.
I. Title.
E902.B37 2003
327.73—dc21

2003014077

ISBN 0-393-32578-4 pbk.

W. W. Norton & Company, Inc.
500 Fifth Avenue, New York, N.Y. 10110
www.wwnorton.com

W. W. Norton & Company Ltd.
Castle House, 75/76 Wells Street, London W1T 3QT

1 2 3 4 5 6 7 8 9 0

To Willson Barber
brother, friend, artist, citizen

Never, never, never believe any war will be smooth
and easy, or that anyone who embarks on the
strange voyage can measure the tides and hurri-
canes he will encounter. The statesman who yields
to war fever must realize that once the signal is
given, he is no longer the master of policy but the
slave of unforeseeable and uncontrollable events.

—WINSTON CHURCHILL,
My Early Life

Woe unto them that are wise in their own eyes, and
prudent in their own sight! . . .
I also will choose their delusions, and
will bring their fears upon them.

—ISAIAH 5:21, 66:4

Contents

Acknowledgments

THIS BOOK WAS written over a lifetime—and in a great hurry. I studied national security policy as a graduate student in the early 1960s and have remained a student of international affairs throughout my career as a political theorist, and much of what I have learned over this lifetime has found its way into these pages. But the rollout of a new preventive war strategy after 9/11 leading to wars in Afghanistan and Iraq, and the prospect of preemptive moves by an American administration possibly bent on "shock and awe" in Iran, North Korea, and other hostile regimes in the near future, impelled me in the fall of 2002 to embark on a fast-track writing schedule. Because of the very short time I had to write, I am especially grateful for the help I received from my personal research assistant, Josh Karant, whose diligent library and Internet research provided empirical, historical, and bibliographical details of paramount importance. Karant also gave me the benefit of his judgment on substance. I was helped too by the invaluable work of my executive assistant, Katie Roman, and key members of the Democracy Collaborative staff—above all Jill Samuels, Sondra Myers, and Michele Demers. I am very pleased to have completed the work as a principal of the new Democracy Collaborative and among my new colleagues at the University of Maryland. As with my earlier book published by W. W. Norton, my work has benefited by the sharp editorial eye and sound judgment of my editor Alane

Mason, and from the dexterously wielded blue pencil of copyeditor Don Rifkin.

Finally, this book represents the written expression of a political commitment to international law and global democracy that is embodied in CivWorld, the citizens campaign for global democracy (www.civworld.org) with which I feel privileged to be involved. Both the book and the campaign reflect my hope that America will give up its futile attempt to meet fear with fear.

I WRITE IN the spirit of Katharine Lee Bates, who composed the lyrics for "America the Beautiful," and in her poem "England to America" authored this prophetic stanza:

> *And what of thee, O Lincoln's Land? What gloom*
> *Is darkening above the Sunset Sea?*
> *Vowed Champion of Liberty, deplume*
> *Thy war-crest, bow thy knee,*
> *Before God answer thee.*

Preface to the Paperback Edition

Six weary GIs, their arms outstretched, raise Old Glory over a Pacific island called Iwo Jima. A little girl, her face a mask of terror, flees from a rice paddy napalm blast. Jeering Somalis drag a battered body, stripped of its U.S. uniform, across the desert floor. A simple stirring picture tells war's epic story in a snapshot. The Heroic Generation's World War II. Quagmire Vietnam. The fiasco of Somalia. But for the arrogant futility of preventive war and the self-defeating self-delusion of President Bush's Afghan and Iraqi misadventures, one photo is not enough.

Recall two, from the spring of '04: One, flaunting the horror of American body parts swinging from a Fallujah bridge as—greater horror still—supposed allies and friends of America exult. And the second, a grisly set of digital pictures, just a couple of weeks later, displaying all those hooded and naked Iraqi prisoners at Abu Ghraib prison west of Baghdad in postures of degradation and humiliation—their American captors leering into the camera as if they had just pulled off a clever fraternity prank.

Just a year into what was to be a happy story of liberation vindicated, the preventive war strategy was in tatters. It had unraveled more or less along the lines foretold by skeptics in the media, cautious warriors in the Pentagon, and scholarly Islamics in academia well before President Bush took his coalition of the willing roaring into Iraq in quest of nonexistent weapons of mass destruction and the head of Saddam Hussein. The pictures, read aright, rehearse lessons taught by the ancient tragedians: that war, no less than peace, must always be approached with humility and a full sense of the intractability of human affairs; and that hubris is forever its own undoing.

The photos throw into relief this book's key puzzle: exactly why, although America has twice won campaigns against rogue states, those very "successes" constitute failures in the war on terrorism. Why is the democratic United States being decisively defeated in the struggle to win hearts and minds in the world of Islam, on which the outcome of the long-term struggle for democracy will hinge? The answer that emerges: it is impossible to liberate people at the barrel of a gun. Generous intentions cannot redeem imprudent policies and costly consequences.

A year after the invasion of Iraq and several years into the adventure called preventive war, all the evidence suggests that President Bush's strategy has failed. There will be no easy transition to democracy in Baghdad with bordering countries falling like dominoes in a neat democratic row; there will be no permanent pacification of Afghanistan even if Osama is finally caught; there will be no Pax Americana military solution to disorder and tyranny in the nondemocratic world; there will be no gratifying payoff for American goodwill, no kudos for America's self-described liberators; and there will be no decisive victory in the war against terrorism or the battle for enduring national security. Although it has been advanced under liberty's banner, fear's empire cannot and will not reign in liberty's name.

Yet for the same reasons that America continues to embrace preventive war in theory even as it everywhere fails in practice, it continues to misread last spring's raw images, drawing from them the wrong conclusions: that anybody who opposes America in its righteous war on terrorism really is evil incarnate (just look at the evils they perpetrated in Fallujah!); that America's purposes *are* truly righteous (just see how aberrant is the behavior of the guards at Abu Ghraib, a few bad apples who do not "represent" America but are a "stain" on its righteous honor!).[1] But these are not the lessons to be drawn from the pictures by the observant viewer, not the lessons they yield to anyone who knows something of America's dialectical history and of democracy's complex nature.

IT IS THE aim of this book to offer a deeper reading of such images—call it an offshore reading of America by an American who loves his country but has an offshore perspective on its policies. I diagnose and criticize the dangerous and all-too-American notion—not original with President Bush—that the world is a Manichaean battlefield painted in blacks and whites, where Evil and Good confront each other at a series of secular Armageddons. I propose rather a world of somber grays, where the good guys are not all so good after all and the bad guys aren't all so bad. Not angels and monsters but frail, muddling, sometimes noble, often deluded creatures of ambiguity, less dreadful than they secretly fear, perhaps, but never as noble as they publicly boast.

What the pictures from Abu Ghraib in fact attest to is the potential ubiquity of the perverse in human behavior and how easily a

---

[1] The official Washington reaction to the Abu Ghraib abuses was to insist they were "aberrational." At the Congressional hearings, Secretary of Defense Rumsfeld called them "fundamentally un-American," while Army General Lance Smith insisted they were a "distasteful and criminal aberration." Even Democrat Joe Lieberman embraced American exceptionalism, saying "Americans are different" and that the abuses were "not the real America. . . . They are not who we are."

strategy of fear pursued by self-righteous American moralists can unleash that perversity. The rationale for preventive war argued that nations subjected to terrorist attack are no longer accountable to traditional legal and moral norms (such as the obligation to go to war only when attacked). When Donald Rumsfeld worried briefly about the consistency of preventive war and international law before the war in Iraq, President Bush set the tone for everything that followed right up to and including Abu Ghraib: "I don't care what the international lawyers say, we are going to kick some ass."[2] Iraq was not a conventional war, he declared, but a preventive war in a momentous struggle against terrorism, against an axis of evil where anything goes. Following his first address to the nation after 9/11, he said much the same thing to his staff: "I want you all to understand that we are at war and we will stay at war until this is done. Nothing else matters. Everything is available for the pursuit of this war. Any barriers in your way, they're gone."

"Any barriers in your way, they're gone"? So why shouldn't the guards at Abu Ghraib intuit they were loosed of normal restraints? The president had said that "enemy combatants" seized in the war on terrorism held at Guantánomo Bay were not subject to the Geneva Conventions. Were the ill-trained keepers at Abu Ghraib prison really to think their prisoners, also captured in the war on terrorism, any different, even if they had been designated conventional POWs for accounting purposes?

How can American officials be surprised when soldiers recruited as shock troops in securing fear's spreading empire, told they are engaged in a holy struggle against "evil ones," use methods calculated to shock, intimidate, and terrorize their captives? Methods that are in any case widely employed in American prisons where the "evil ones" are at worst street criminals and Americans of

[2] Quoted by Richard A. Clarke, *Against All Enemies* (New York: Free Press, 2004), pp. 23–24.

color?[3] Even under ordinary circumstances, psychologists have shown over and over again that in what were supposed to be simulations, civilians asked to play the role of prison guards or interrogators tend to abandon humane norms and with a quite astonishing ease fall into behavior verging on torture.[4] Yet many continue to insist that men and women of goodwill (Americans by definition!) are incapable of producing bad results (un-American by definition!). What happened at Abu Ghraib, what happened to all the uncounted civilians killed during Iraq's liberation, what happened in the "collateral damage" inflicted on Afghanistan was wholly unintended and thus not to be entered in America's moral ledger. What an unassailable morality this is, for it cannot be refuted by the facts. In the scathing satire of *Daily Show* ironist Rob Corddry: "Remember, it's not important that we did torture those people. What's important is that we're not the kind of people who would torture those people."

The truth is America, like other nations, will be judged and should judge itself by what it does, not what it says it does. Like other peoples, Americans are a mixture of the noble and the base, of daunting aspirations and recurring failures to live up to them:

[3] "Physical and sexual abuse of prisoners, similar to what has been uncovered in Iraq," wrote Fox Butterfield in the *New York Times*, "takes place in American prisons with little public knowledge or concern, according to corrections officials, inmates and human rights advocates" ("Mistreatment of Prisoners Is Called Routine in the U.S.," *New York Times*, May 5, 2004, p. A11).

[4] Stanley Milgram's famous experiment in 1971 showed that a majority of players were willing to administer apparently painful (even fatal) shocks to subjects when urged to do so by an authority figure (see *Obedience to Authority: An Experimental View* [New York: Harper and Row, 1974]), while in an experiment at Stanford in 1974, Stanford University psychologist Philip Zimbardo found that teams of pretend prisoners and guards turned so quickly into torturers and victims (showing some of the same inclinations to sexual abuse exhibited at Abu Ghraib) that he had to terminate the experiment just five days into what was to have been a two-week simulation.

the first great modern republic, and for more than eighty years a republic of slaves. A nation dedicated to liberty, but one slow to bring it to a majority of its own people. A reluctant empire less callous than most, but deadly enough to those it occupies, even as it pursues a campaign against terror in Iraq variously called "enduring freedom" and "shock and awe."

The quest for freedom must be pursued with humility, and humility demands restraint. James Madison taught that to arrange a constitution around a jaded view of human nature was a safer bet than counting on our nobler side. American liberty owes a great debt to America's distrust of power—of its own power. Why then do we think others should trust us because we claim to be their liberators? Or that privates and sergeants running riot in Iraqi prisons are guilty while a defense secretary and a president who say "anything goes" in the war on terrorism are innocent?

THEN THERE WERE those other pictures, the ones depicting the wrenching slaughter of the Blackwater contractors in Fallujah: a portrait of evil terrorists who slew their innocent victims and vanished. These too were not fully decoded, however. For those who milled about grinning and cheering in front of the desecrated corpses were not the killers themselves, long gone, but ordinary Iraqis who had not participated in the actual murders. What was so disturbing in the graphic images of exultant teens dancing on the corpses was exactly what was most dismaying in the pictures broadcast from much of the Muslim world after 9/11—pictures of ordinary people reveling in extraordinary mayhem not because they were terrorists but because they hated America.

This is the question that has vexed Americans ever since 9/11: *why do they hate us?* Not the few who kill, but the many who shout for joy at the killings? Not the adversaries whose interests are obviously endangered by American power, but the "friends" who are supposed to be grateful for its exercise in their name? How could men and women who might be loath to justify terrorism in principle, and certainly would themselves never engage in acts of terrorism, welcome such barbarous assaults? Why are Shiites—those explicitly "liberated" from Saddam's brutalities by the American invasion—also at war with the "forces of liberation," seeming to prefer the reempowerment of their erstwhile Sunni torturers to continued occupation by the liberators? How is it that though we came to liberate and democratize them, the Iraqis—and yes, quite a few Afghani and all too many Saudis and Egyptians and western Europeans and American Muslims too—wish upon us (though they are not "savages") only gruesome death and continue to assassinate the "sovereign" governors we have installed in our place?

The answer lies in the futility of fear as a democratic weapon against terrorism. "Shock and awe" is terrorism's stock and trade: democracy takes it up only by risking its liberal essence. The sober Cold Warrior Zbigniew Brzezinski confirms this reality, observing recently that the "shock and awe tactic hailed by the strategists of the 'revolution in military affairs' finds its counterpoint in the paralyzing panic that the weak at low cost can unleash among the powerful."[5]

Why do they hate us? In a word, our hypocrisy. The high moralism of our intentions conjoined with the harsh consequences of our deeds. Horrendous outcomes? Not us. Americans don't do such things. The twin pillars of the administration's antiterror strategy, preventive war and democratization, turn out in practice to be fundamentally at odds, a standing reminder to the world of American hypocrisy. Such hypocrisy has forever been the Achilles' heel of impe-

[5] Zbigniew Brzezinski, *The Choice: Global Domination or Global Leadership* (New York: Basic Books, 2004), p. 45.

rial democracies. In 1917, another "liberator," British general Stanley Maude, stood at the doors of Baghdad and announced, "Our armies do not come into your cities and lands as conquerors or enemies, but as liberators."[6] Nearly ninety years later, President Bush proclaims Maude-like: "I believe the United States is the beacon for freedom in the world. . . . And I believe I have a duty to free people."[7]

PREVENTIVE WAR PREVENTS not terrorism but democracy. The second part of this book shows how America under Bush has misconceived what it means to be democratic and what it takes to get there. While I am sympathetic with the basic claim that democratization is a valuable weapon in the war on terrorism, if the tactic of democratization (what I call preventive democracy) is to succeed, the tactics of preventive war must be abandoned. For even as preventive war eliminates terrorists, it enlarges the population of tacit supporters without whom terrorists cannot operate. The wild card in America's dangerous game of preventive war turns out to be those unwilling beneficiaries of our democratic largesse who refuse to be grateful and whose raging opposition amounts to a kind of tacit terrorism—a yielding to terrorism's rationale that does not engage directly in its methods. It is not terrorists but tacit supporters who, in the midst of the regions we have putatively liberated,

[6] Niall Ferguson, quoting General Maude on the eve of a three-year failed war aimed at "liberating" Mesopotamia from the dominion of the Ottomans, in his *Colossus: The Price of American Empire* (New York: Penguin Press, 2004), p. 200. In making the comparison between 1917 and 2003, Ferguson observes that "in both cases, Anglophone troops had been able to sweep from the south of the country to the capital in a matter of weeks. In both cases, their governments disclaimed any desire to rule Iraq directly. . . . In both cases, imposing law and order proved much harder than achieving the initial military victory."

[7] As quoted in Bob Woodward, *Plan of Attack* (New York: Simon & Schuster, 2004), pp. 86–87.

have established safe zones for the active killers. Neither killers nor terrorists themselves, the keepers of the safe zones harbor hatreds and resentments that fuel the active terrorists' war-making. They are the "reserve population" from whom the actual fighters and suicide bombers can be drawn. They are why we can't "decapitate" terrorism by removing leaders or arresting individual evildoers or overthrowing evil regimes. They are why Sharon's iron fist can mercilessly pummel Palestinian terrorists without destroying the Palestinian insurgency on which the terrorists depend.

Think of the major terrorist figures still on the loose: many appear still to reside in countries and areas under the control of the United States or its allies (if not actually inside Europe and the United States, where the perpetrators of 9/11 had dwelled for years prior to committing their acts of terror). If Abu Musab al-Zarqawi operated alone with a tiny cell of supporters in Iraq, he would have been caught long ago. If Osama bin Laden was a solitary mass murderer, his capture would have been assured. But these extraordinary fanatics have secured the support of ordinary believers. They make vast safe houses out of their tacit support base, turning whole regions into "safe provinces" in Afghanistan and "safe cities" in Iraq. It was not a network of tunnels that offered an escape route to the "high-value target" supposedly cornered in a much-touted Pakistani offensive in the late winter of 2003–2004, it was a network of tribesmen who wanted to see him go free. In fact much of Afghanistan and perhaps all of Pakistan remain "safe" countries for Osama.

The logic of the preventive war strategy has been to posit that a tiny coterie of evil zealots "sponsored" by a handful of rogue nations vulnerable to preemptive intervention were responsible for the horrendous deeds of 9/11, for the subsequent evils in Casablanca and Bali and Riyadh and Istanbul and Madrid, as well as for the ongoing assaults against civilians in Iraq and Saudi Arabia. But the harsh reality is that such deeds are not possible in the absence of a wider sea of support that protects and nourishes the evildoers, and that the sea in which terrorists swim is not a league of evil states (tyrannical states generally fear terrorism as the Baathists in Iraq did and the Baathists in Syria still do) but a global, nonstate collective of angry citizens, marginalized young men, religious congregations under siege, and cultures imperiled by modernity. These are the tacit terrorists of Jihad for whom hypocrisy is a spur to resistance.

MAO TSE-TUNG, the architect of modern guerilla war, understood that his insurgents fighting the Kuomintang Nationalist government in China could swim only when buoyed up by the sea of "the people." Terrorism flourishes and reproduces itself despite America's overwhelming military and intelligence capabilities and despite the military defeat of sponsoring states because it has a far wider constituency than we are willing to acknowledge, and by no means among "evildoers" alone. To acknowledge this would be to acknowledge that terrorism is a symptom of global systemic disorders, and that until those disorders are addressed (whether or not America is their cause), America will not be greeted as a liberator anywhere and the horrors visited on individual Americans and other allied supporting states or even well-meaning humanitarian workers will continue.

Humanitarian efforts have themselves been compromised by the false linkage posited by America between the marketization of the economy and the democratization of the polity. The neoliberal ideology of privatization appears to President Bush to define democracy. But to the Iraqis and many others it appears to define hypocritical neocolonialism. One of Paul Bremer's first acts in Iraq in the summer of 2003 was to announce that the energy sector, heavy industry, and the media would all be privatized as a prelude to, and condition for, a democratic constitution.[8] Yet the choice between a public or a private economy is perhaps the most important democratic choice a people can make, and by making that choice for the Iraqis the Americans effectively stole from them a marker of their sovereignty. This confounding of privatization and democracy is one of the errors addressed in the second part of this volume, and helps explain why the road to democracy in Iraq has been so difficult to construct. In fact, there will be no democracy in Iraq as long as its citizens prefer chaos to an American occupation that appears to be an exercise in market colonialism. There will be no peace in Afghanistan as long as tacit terrorists there and in Pakistan provide Mullah Omar and Osama safe passage, because life under the imperial economy feels oppressive rather than liberating.

To be sure, the United States is winning the war against rogue states, although this is less because of its overwhelming military superiority than because it has worked with friends and allies to bring economic incentives, political suasion, and law to bear on former rogue nations such as Libya and Sudan. It now appears likely that North Korea, the axis of evil's most dangerous member, may actually be brought to heel by economic manipulation and smart diplomacy (e.g., working with China) rather than military intimidation and smart bombs. It has also made progress in prosecuting terrorist cells, again largely as a consequence of the multilateral cooperation that grew out of the universal sympathy produced by the horrors of 9/11. But it is losing the struggle—it is barely engaging in the struggle—against terrorism's tacit network of support among those who are themselves not terrorists. This growing network cannot be vanquished by war and occupation, for the deep hatreds of terrorism's tacit constituents arise not out of fundamen-

---

[8] The failures on the ground since that time have forced Bremer to postpone privatization, but it remains a crucial part of the American ideology of democratization.

talist zealotry but out of grievances rooted in humiliation, poverty, hopelessness, and cultural resentment—forces that produce enemies more intractable than teens wearing explosive belts and terrorist cells planning urban mayhem. We need not sympathize with those who revel in our misfortune, but we need to understand them and address the toxic combination of powerlessness, resentment, and humiliation that drives them. The axis of evil can be overcome by prudent intelligence and brute force. The axis of anger—far more encompassing—is difficult to fathom and still harder to address. But until we begin to do so, our courageous troops and billions of dollars notwithstanding, the hatred will abide, the gruesome scenes of carnage will multiply, and the war on terrorism will find no resolution.

There is little satisfaction in being right, when it is your own country that is proved wrong. In 1995, in *Jihad vs. McWorld*, I warned that the American world of commercial secularism, advanced with such aggressive self-certainty, was on a collision course with fundamentalist Islam and other antimodern movements around the world in ways that might one day devastate democracy. I wrote again last year in this book that America was still on a collision course with history and that the beacon of democracy the world once most admired was fast becoming the maker of war the world most fears. From Kabul and Karachi to Fallujah and Baghdad, the disastrous consequences are now evident. Whether or not President Bush survives the November 2004 election, his policies of preventive war have left the United States in a desperate condition where it hardly has viable choices.[9] Precipitous

---

[9] Even in Afghanistan, where some will argue preventive war was justified, there is little reason to believe the Bush administration policies have worked. Seymour M. Hersh notes that a year and a half after the war there, "the Taliban are still a force in many parts of Afghanistan, and the country continues to provide safe haven for members of Al Qaeda. . . . [L]ocal warlords . . .

withdrawal from the zones it precipitously occupied means the acknowledgment of defeat and can only encourage America's predatory adversaries. But continued occupation will compound the costs and dangers, stretching resources and creating impassioned new Jihadic enemies. The preventive war policy has done the worst thing any policy can do: it has rendered further policy choices nearly impossible. And it has given a bad name to the democracy in whose name it rationalizes its foolish tactics.

Democracy not only seems a more distant prospect today in Afghanistan and Iraq than a year ago, but its reputation in Africa and Latin America is suffering, partly as a result of the fiascos in the American war zones, and partly because of the confounding of democracy and market economics that have been the hallmark of Bush policies in those zones and elsewhere in the world. A United Nations report on Latin America warns that people there are losing faith in democracy, with 58 percent agreeing that leaders should "go beyond the law" if they have to and 56 percent insisting that "economic development is more important than democracy."[10] To far too many people beyond American shores, President Bush's use of democracy as a rationale for preventive adventurism looks more and more like the hucksterism of a cynical neocolonial power.

Even on the American right, faith in Bush's democratization

---

effectively control the provinces. . . . Heroin production is soaring, and, outside of Kabul and a few other cities, people are terrorized by violence and crime" ("The Other War," *The New Yorker*, April 12, 2004).

[10]Warren Hoge, "Latin America Losing Hope in Democracy, Report Says," *New York Times*, April 22, 2004, p. A3. The report to which Hoge refers warns that "it must be recognized that both in terms of progress towards democracy and in terms of the economic and social dynamic, the region is experiencing a period of change that in many cases takes the form of widespread crisis . . . characterized by change, by the concentration of wealth and by the increasing internationalization of politics" (United Nations Development Programme, "Democracy in Latin America," UNDP, 2004).

strategies are flagging. Not long ago, William F. Buckley's *National Review* published an editorial under the headline "An End to Illusion," in which the Bush administration was said to have "a dismaying capacity to believe its own public relations" and was said to have failed to grasp "the difficulty of implanting democracy in alien soil" in what "is still fundamentally a tribal society," while other critics have lambasted the "Wilsonian" idealism of Bush's approach (as embodied in Bill Kristol's defense of it in *The Weekly Standard*, for example).[11] In truth, the choice today is not between some discredited Wilsonian form of "democratic universalism" (foolish utopianism) on the one hand and cynical neorealism that prefers isolationism to the advance of democracy on the other hand. The real choice is between the hubris of preventive war advanced under the cynical guise of democracy and the cautious realism of preventive democracy as the only effective response to terrorism.

In a world of interdependence, arrogant unilateralism and knee-jerk opposition to multilateral treaties and international law imperil rather than enhance national security. Going it alone in Iraq (paper "coalition" notwithstanding) won America a quick military success but now assures it a slow and excruciating civic failure.

Preventive war and democracy are fundamentally incompatible. The first requires unilateralism, brute force, and a willingness to do battle on fear's own turf. The second demands cooperation, law, and a readiness to pay the price of staying on the turf of openness and transparency. Democracy need not forgo force of arms, but it cannot make force of arms its primary tool or abdicate the democratic standards that always ground and limit force in free societies. The fear inspired by military power is a convenient and, in the

---

[11] David D. Kirkpatrick, "Lack of Resolution in Iraq Finds Conservatives Divided," *New York Times*, April 19, 2004, p. A21.

short term, effective instrument. But fear is terrorism's chief weapon, its only resource, and in the long term democracy cannot win the war with terrorism if it fights on terrorism's turf. Democracy depends on partnership and law and both excels in using them and benefits by their spread. America must choose—preventive war or democracy? It cannot have both.

FEAR'S

EMPIRE

Introduction

It is better to be feared than loved.
Machiavelli, The Prince

THE UNITED STATES, destiny's longtime darling, is on a collision course with history. Insulated from the old world by two centuries of near mythic independence but stunned today by a sudden consciousness of vulnerability, America is failing to read the message of mandatory interdependence that defines the new twenty-first-century world.

Terrorists otherwise bereft of power have bored into the American imagination, seeding its recesses and crannies with anxieties for which the technicolor terror alert codes are unsettling indicators. Yet in its approach to confronting terrorism, whether prosecuting wars abroad or pursuing security at home, America has conjured the very fear that is terrorism's principal weapon. Its leaders pursue a reckless militancy aimed at establishing an American empire of fear more awesome than any the terrorists can conceive. Promising to disarm every adversary, to deploy "the mother of all bombs" and remove the taboo against the tactical use of nuclear weapons, to shock and awe enemies and friends alike into global submission, the beacon of democracy the world once most admired has abruptly become the maker of war the world most fears.[1]

---

[1] The "mother of all bombs" (technically, the Massive Ordnance Air Blast, or MOAB) is the Defense Department's new 21,000-pound "conventional"

Some may think this is all to the good. The issue for America and the world alike is not only whether America can deploy new strategies of preventive war and still stay true to its defining democratic values, and hence remain on affectionate terms with its global neighbors; it is whether these strategies can actually succeed in securing it against terrorism. No nation can be expected to sacrifice its safety on the altar of its nobler aspirations. Machiavelli taught the Prince it was better to be feared than loved. America may have drawn from 9/11 the same lesson. But is fear America's best ally? Are Afghanistan and Iraq to become benchmarks for a successful global strategy of security through intimidation?

Not in an era of interdependence. Not when going it alone invites failure. Not when terrorism has exposed the frailty of sovereignty and the obsolescence of once proud declarations of independence. If 9/11 teaches a lesson about fear's potency, it also tells a story of the insufficiencies of military power. If the techno-blitzkrieg in Iraq teaches a lesson about military power's enduring relevance, it also tells a story of its limits as an instrument of democratization. Yet in responding to terrorism's disregard for national frontiers, the United States has reached for increasingly obsolete military strategies associated with a traditional sovereignty it no longer fully possesses. Seeking a safer world, it has systematically undermined collective security. Reacting to global lawlessness, the nation has vacillated between appealing to law and undermining it, between employing international institutions and defying them. It has invoked a right to unilateral action, preventive

---

bomb; the Pentagon under President Bush has hinted that there are circumstances under which it might contemplate a "first use" of tactical nuclear weapons. See, for example, the *Newsweek* cover story "Why America Scares the World," March 24, 2003.

war, and regime change that undermines the international framework of cooperation and law of which it was once the chief architect—when this framework, alone, can overcome terrorist anarchy. President Bush's war on terrorism may or may not be just, may or may not conform to American values, but more important, in the form it has been pursued, its military successes notwithstanding, it cannot and will not defeat terrorism.

From the plague of HIV to global warming, from global media monopolies to international crime syndicates, every emerging feature of the interdependent world calls for America to look outward; instead, it blinks and turns inward, gazing overseas only to fix its baleful eye on "enemy" targets defined by an elusive war on terrorism and quixotically selected "rogue states" meant to stand in for terrorists too difficult to locate and destroy. Although it is the "model" democratic society, America often acts with plutocratic disdain for the demands of global equality, condemning a shadowy "axis of evil" while ignoring an all too visible axis of inequality. It has elected to pursue a national security strategy of preventive war under conditions that cry out for a national security strategy I call "preventive democracy." Although it is the emblematic multicultural nation, it shows little patience for cultural diversity or religious heterogeneity, especially where they appear to threaten American ideals or to lie outside the compass of the American imagination. It believes that, even as it continues to support dictatorship in nations it regards as friends, it can impose democracy on vanquished enemies at the barrel of a gun. It thinks privatized markets and aggressive consumerism freed of democratic constraints are what it means to forge democracy; it believes others can establish democracy overnight by importing American institutions it took centuries to nurture and grow in the United States. America's current foreign policies for war and for peace, for overthrowing tyranny and for establishing democracy, rest on a defective under-standing of the consequences of interdependence and the charac-ter of democracy. Thus does fear's empire produce an empire of fear inimical to both liberty and security.

American militancy is reflected in and perhaps exacerbated by President Bush's missionary zeal in prosecuting the war on terror—a kind of *High Noon* cowboy righteousness that even friends of the White House have associated with the president's tendencies to be "impatient and quick to anger; sometimes glib, even dogmatic; often uncurious and as a result ill-informed."[2] But the American response to terrorism is more than just a question of presidential tem-per. Americans generally choose representative commanders in chief who reflect their own anxieties and aspirations at a given moment in history. Both national parties and leading opinion elites have sup-ported the idea that fear can only be defeated by fearsomeness. While the world trembles, Americans release their own cold fear in shivers of applause for a militant Americanism punctuated by "USA! USA!"

The world beyond America always used to be more than a world away. With it crowding America's doorstep today, Americans gather nervously in the parlor hoping they can secure their safety by lock-ing the doors and thrusting their intimidating smart weapons out of well-secured gunports. Fearful of the otherness of the world, and oddly oblivious to the fact that they embody that otherness in their own diversity, they look to coerce hostile parts of the planet into sub-mission with a strong-willed militancy. Friends and allies follow along

---

[2] A portrait drawn by former Bush speechwriter David Frum, who gets partial credit for coining the phrase "axis of evil" (he coined "axis of hate," which became "axis of evil," presumably to better accommodate President Bush's evangelical moralism). Frum believes Bush's virtues—"decency, honesty, rec-titude, courage, and tenacity"—outweigh the vices cited above. See David Frum, *The Right Man: The Surprise Presidency of George W. Bush* (New York: Random House, 2003), p. 272.

reluctantly because America's power is not to be denied, even where the realities of interdependence mean it is unlikely to triumph.

America's world has then become a place far more perilous and perplexing than Americans have ever known before—a puzzling new world of doubt and danger, a world nominally pledged to the democracy Americans believe they embody, but a world no longer always willing to believe America's claim to embody it. Feeling less than trusted and too little loved by that world, Americans may intervene more but trust it little and love it less in return. The useful myths (they once functioned as verities) by which the last century's costly hot and cold wars were bravely fought and decisively won— American autonomy, American virtue, American democracy, and American innocence—are reasserted with patriotic ardor at home, even as they are deemed hollow and hypocritical abroad. America's world is no longer America's world. It is at risk of becoming at once a willing colony and the capital of fear's spreading empire.

AMERICAN HEGEMONY IS not in question. After all, "the military, economic and political power of the United States makes the rest of the world look Lilliputian."[3] It is, Michael Ignatieff reminds us, "the only nation that polices the world through five global military commands; maintains more than a million men and women at arms on four continents; deploys carrier battle groups on watch in every ocean, guarantees the survival of countries from Israel to South Korea; drives the wheels of global trade and commerce; and fills the hearts and minds of an entire planet with its dreams and desires."[4] Walter Russell Mead raises the ante still further: "The

[3] Tim Wiener, "Mexico's Influence in Security Council Decision May Help Its Ties with U.S.," *New York Times*, November 9, 2002, p. A11.

[4] Michael Ignatieff, "The Burden," *New York Times Magazine*, January 5, 2002, p. 22.

United States," he writes, admiringly, "is not only the sole global power, its values inform a global consensus, and it dominates to an unprecedented degree the formation of the first truly global civilization our planet has known."[5]

Spending more on its military budget ($350 billion and climbing, not including the costs of the war with Iraq) than the next fifteen or so defense high spenders put together (all of America's allies together spend less than $220 million), and deploying high-tech armaments no nation can match, America can crush those nations it regards as enemies almost at will. Picking off a random terrorist with a missile fired from an unmanned Predator aircraft in a no-name desert here, bringing down an unfriendly regime by military intimidation there, prepared to go to war on a "preventive" basis well before an actual act of aggression is committed against America most anywhere, the United States is a formidable adversary. Having helped bring down the Soviet Union by exhausting it in an arms race, and then having used its own weapons to defeat conventional ones in Afghanistan and Iraq in wars so lopsided they scarcely deserve the name, it knows it is without military peers in the manufacture, deployment, and use of armaments, including those awesome weapons of mass destruction it has decided its potential enemies cannot be permitted to develop. No wonder President Bush thinks that if Americans have to, they can prevail even if they are "the only ones left"—a willing coalition of one.

Yet its power makes the United States weak even as it makes it strong, leaving it unloved by those it "saves" (South Korea has shown little more affection for the United States recently than its enemy to the north), resented by its allies (the 2002 German election was won by a candidate who came from behind in the polls by

[5] Walter Russell Mead, *American Foreign Policy and How It Changed the World* (New York: Alfred A. Knopf, 2002), p. 10.

categorically refusing to support America's polices in Iraq), and despised even more than it is feared by those it effects to conquer (a belligerent North Korea; an ambivalent, sometimes sullen Iraq that did not—as it was supposed to—altogether welcome the U.S. invasion). In its unprecedented power lies an unprecedented vulnerability: for it must repeatedly extend the compass of its power to preserve what it already has, and so is almost by definition always overextended. "To secure my turf," noted the powerful landholder, "all I need is the land adjacent to my own." It must count as friends all who pretend not to be its enemies, so that its allies are more often the enemies of its enemies rather than its real friends. To be opposed to the United States is to belong to, if not the axis of evil, at least to the bad guys; to support the United States is to be a good guy, even if the supportive regime is authoritarian or even tyrannical, as in the case of close American friends and allies such as Egypt, Saudi Arabia, Pakistan, and Zimbawe. It is hardly a wonder then that the United States obsesses over minor league rogue states like Libya, Somalia, Cuba, and Iraq, whose threat to American interests, even when magnified by interdependence, is nominal. It has the resources to field military forces around the globe and to fight several wars at once, but it cannot protect its own headquarters at the Pentagon or the cathedral of capitalism in Manhattan because interdependence permits the weak to use the forces of the strong jujitsu style to overcome them. Fear is terrorism's only weapon, but fear is a far more potent weapon against those who live in hope and prosperity than those who live in despair with nothing to lose.

Moreover, because the nearly invisible, highly mobile agents that oversee terrorism are not nation-states and can melt away and reappear in multiple venues, they are little affected by America's vaunted military might. The United States can strike down whole nations, but terrorist cells and their ever-morphing leaders are left standing. They know that fear is their ally: in the words of Anwar Aziz, who was an early suicide bomber in Gaza in 1993, "battles for Islam are won not through the gun but by striking fear into the enemy's heart."[6] And even were they to fear death, what have terrorists to fear from armies that cannot find them? Donald Rumsfeld, as enthusiastic a proponent of preventive war as America has produced, worries about the elusiveness of terrorist cells. "The people who do this don't lose, don't have high-value targets," he acknowledges. "They have networks and fanaticism."[7] Why then, one might ask, are we to believe that counterstate preventive war strategy can ever really work against terrorism, even when it "works" to punish or modify unfriendly regimes?

Even as America tries to secure itself against terrorism (one form of the new global anarchy) through sovereign dominion, the international market economy (another form of the new global anarchy) eats away at the very idea of sovereignty. Although it has made its world over in its own image, the United States is hardpressed to control its own economy because interdependence permits capital, jobs, and investment to move where they will—American sovereignty notwithstanding. America can spread a pop cultural civilization of movies, music, software, fast food, and infor-

---

[6] Cited by Avisahi Margalit in his revealing essay "The Suicide Bombers," *New York Review of Books*, January 16, 2003.

[7] Cited by Bob Woodward, *Bush at War* (New York: Simon & Schuster, 2002), p. 89. Since Woodward's method is not so much dubious as it is inscrutable (there is no way to check his attributions or many of his direct citations), I leave it to the reader to determine their veracity. I take their cumulative force to be of relevance even where I distrust them one by one. Many of those I cite here are from public speeches or speeches made public, but others depend on the reader's trust. For good reasons not to trust Woodward, see the reviews of *Bush at War* (from different sides of the political spectrum) by Eric Alterman, "War and Leaks," *American Prospect*, December 30, 2002; and Edward N. Luttwak, "Gossip from the War Room," *Los Angeles Times Book Review*, December 1, 2002.

mation technology across the world until the world is reborn as McWorld, but it cannot control the blowback that is Jihad: for interdependence gives to Jihad means to confront McWorld (global terrorism!) no less impressive than the means McWorld possesses to confront Jihad (global markets!). Indeed, they are, in one sense, the very same means in that both are founded on a global anarchy that both promote.[8]

There are multiple pressure points where American hegemony and global interdependence can be found colliding. These include the disturbing inequalities of the north/south divide, the anarchic marketization of the global economy, and the pervasive homogenization of cultures that has followed the spread of McWorld. But no point of collision has been more dramatic or more perilous than the one disclosed by evolving American strategic doctrine.

Terrorism's successes pose in brutal terms to America and the world straightforward questions: Can the United States really remedy the pathologies of a global interdependence it helped create, and which has eroded the sovereignty on which it depends, by deploying the traditional strategies of the sovereign state—above all, overweening military power in the supposedly innovative form of preventive war? Can the old regimes born in the eighteenth and nineteenth centuries contend with the globalized malevolence they have inadvertently helped to create—without first creating benevolent forms of interdependence that replace global disorder with lawful order? Can international governance come about through the anarchic processes of markets and war? Can fear defeat fear? Can a politics of nation-states (America vs. Iraq, South Korea vs. North Korea, Palestine vs. Israel) contend with a world comprised more and more by a wide variety of nonstate actors (al-Qaeda, Shell, Greenpeace, OPEC, Bertelsmann, Hezbollah)?

[8] See my *Jihad vs. McWorld*, rev. ed. (New York: Random House, 2001).

His country under attack from what was, in effect, a terrorist nongovernmental organization (al-Qaeda), President Bush sought vengeance on "states that harbored terrorism." This impelled him into a strategy that targeted Afghanistan and then Iraq (and perhaps in time North Korea and Syria and Iran), even as terrorists moved freely from Afghanistan to Yemen and Sudan; from the unruly and ungovernable mountain provinces of Afghanistan to the unruly and ungovernable provinces of Pakistan; from the Middle East to Africa and Southeast Asia, to Indonesia and the Philippines. In fact, ironically enough, as America and Europe exported their forces to confront terrorism in the Third World, Third World terrorists have continued to roost in England and Germany and in New England and New Jersey and Florida as well. Such states too must be counted (though obviously he did not) among those harboring terrorists on whom President Bush promised to wreak a terrible vengeance. (To date, New Jersey and Florida are not on the hit list—although some would argue that the encroachment of homeland security and the Patriot Act on civil liberties within the United States has effectively put them there.)

Yet while terrorism appears an impressive display of brute power, it is in fact a strategy of fear rather than force, of weakness rather than strength. Donald Rumsfeld likes to quote Al Capone's lines about how "you will get more with a kind word and a gun than with a kind word alone," but in doing so he is playing the terrorist's game on the terrorists' turf. Indeed, because fear is terrorism's only weapon, the terrorist's primary job (as with an infectious agent) is merely to initiate the contagion. The contaminated body's immune system does the rest as the body struggles to neutralize the infection by making war on its own infected systems. Hence, the American government was compelled to close down its commercial aviation system for a number of days and hem it in with crippling security provisions more or less permanently in response to the

9/11 hijackings.[9] The aviation industry has been in shock ever since. The hijackers closed down the stock market not only by destroying facilities in the World Trade Center but by inspiring fear—a kind of speculative immune reaction to the attacks, doing its own damage more effectively than al-Qaeda could have. The stock market has yet to recover. Before the war in Iraq began, the government closed off pedestrian access in front of the White House and, with unintended irony, walled in the Liberty Bell in Philadelphia.

Terrorism's strategic jujitsu cannot win other than by leveraging others into losing, overcoming them by dint of their own forceful momentum. The diabolical intelligence behind the World Trade Center and Pentagon attacks was evident in the crude but demonically imaginative use of passenger planes as lethal firebombs by men armed otherwise only with box cutters. It is even more visible a year or two later in the way Americans anxiously watch their own government's color-coded signals announcing today's levels of risk to determine how safe they are supposed to feel—and feeling deeply unsafe precisely because their level of fear is now color-coded for them. One might ask whether any terrorist can have spread fear more effectively than the American government inadvertently has done as it dutifully passes on random threats against unspecified targets and warns that further attacks are a virtual certainty. When the terror alert was once again raised to "high" in spring 2003 following terrorist attacks in Riyadh and Casablanca (despite the "victory" against terrorism supposedly represented by the overthrow of Saddam Hussein), a "knowledgeable U.S. official"

---

[9] President Bush had an instinctive grasp of this and on 9/11 tried to get commercial aviation in the air again: "We won't be held hostage," he said, "we'll fly at noon tomorrow" (Woodward, *Bush at War*, p. 27). In fact, it was another three days before flights were resumed, with the Federal Aviation Administration inadvertently doing the terrorists' work for them.

warned that the so-called intelligence chatter and intercepted mes-
sages contained "reasonably spooky stuff," Halloween in May.[10]

Terrorism can induce a country to scare itself into a kind of
paralysis. It disempowers the powerful by provoking an anxiety that
disables capacity. It turns active citizens into fretful spectators.
There is nothing more conducive to fear than inaction. Take, for
example, the anthrax scare in the United States a few weeks after
9/11. Anthrax itself, although it cost five precious lives, did minimal
systemic damage. Indeed, it was probably the work of a disgruntled
American laboratory employee rather than a foreign terrorist. But
because it involved the universal postal service system, the threat
generated a nationwide fear that devastated the country's collective
sense of security.

Names can contribute to the sense of fear. There is even something slippery and distracting in the term *weapons of mass
destruction* (WMD), since the phrase passes easily from the certain and widely recognized mass devastation associated with
nuclear weapons to the far less predictable outcomes associated
with biological and chemical weapons. The 1995 sarin attack
launched by the Japanese terrorist group Aum Shinrikyo in the
Tokyo subway was technically a chemical weapons attack and
hence to be classified as a "weapons of mass destruction" incident.
Though thousands were affected, only twelve people perished,
and commentators have since noted that this attack demonstrated
the extraordinary difficulties of using chemical weapons even in
closed spaces like subway systems. The anthrax incidents in the
United States affecting U.S. post offices, broadcast studios, and
government offices were biological attacks—instances of
"weapons of mass destruction" at work. But while they certainly
spread fear far and wide (in part because of how they were

[10] Cited in Jeanne Meserve, "Cities Respond Differently to Terror Alert,"
CNN.com, May 21, 2003.

depicted by the government and the pandering media), actual casualties were minimal. Is it really useful to regard such incidents as instances of the deployment of weapons of mass destruction (recently modified to read "weapons of mass terror" by Deputy Secretary of Defense Paul Wolfowitz)? Surely "conventional" weapons—including napalm, cluster bombs, and land mines—have taken far more civilian lives in earlier conflicts (though the United States is not even a signatory to the International Land Mine Ban Treaty).[11]

Could it be that the intention of the new term *weapons of mass destruction* is less to create a coherent new military classification than to reinforce a strained logic of preventive war so that it can be applied to sovereign states rather than terrorist organizations—states that do not yet have the nuclear weapons that might justify preventive interdiction? (That is, if the possible presence of such weapons, as in North Korea,[12] did not make such interdiction too costly.)[13] Henry Sokolski, executive director of the Nonproliferation

[11] There are some reasonable arguments for America's reluctance, since it deploys more troops around the world than any other nation and utilizes land mines as an inexpensive protection for outnumbered garrisons; moreover, it has a good record of picking up its mines when it leaves. But the point here is that weapons that are regularly used with far greater casualties than any chemical or biological weapons have caused are excluded from the term *weapons of mass destruction*, while other less historically damaging weapons are included—presumably because they help make the American case for preventive war.

[12] North Korea apparently has several nuclear weapons. It is widely believed it is beginning production for fissionable material for many more.

[13] This is certainly the logic of some supporters of preventive war, including Tod Lindberg, who has acknowledged with astonishing frankness that in order for preventive war to work as deterrence, "one must be able to prevail in teaching the lesson one wants learned"—something only a uniquely armed nuclear hegemon like the United States can do. In this sense, Lindberg adds altogether appropriately, "preemption or prevention cannot be said to have superseded deterrence. Rather, preemption is the violent reestablishment of the terms of deterrence" (Tod Lindberg, "Deterrence and Prevention," *Weekly Standard*, February 3, 2003, p. 25).

Policy Education Center in Washington, has noted that Syria, Egypt, Turkey, and Algeria are all potential developers of nuclear weapons in that part of the world, while Taiwan, South Korea, and Japan are capable of doing so in Asia.[14]

In fact, the term *weapons of mass destruction* was used as early as 1937 to refer to Germany's new bombing techniques in the Spanish Civil War, and became closely associated with "atomic bombs and similar weapons of mass destruction" immediately after World War II.[15] Throughout the Cold War, it was used to refer to nuclear (plutonium) and thermonuclear (hydrogen) bombs. The use of chemical agents like mustard gas, on the other hand, has been a threat since World War I, and is of course the subject of the Chemical and Biological Weapons Convention—about which, despite its constant references to WMD, the United States been remarkably ambivalent, unhappy with inspection provisions that might encroach on American sovereignty. Only after 9/11 has the term *weapons of mass destruction* been used to elide the differences between the original nuclear and thermonuclear weapons of mass destruction and biological and chemical agents which have historically never exacted the casualties associated with conventional bombing (cluster bombs or napalm, for example) or even land mines. Indeed, prior to 9/11, "as of July 1999, the largest number of casualties in a single terrorist incident were the 329 passengers killed in the explosion of an Air India jumbo jet off the coast

[14] Henry Sokolski, "Two, Three, Many North Koreas," *Weekly Standard*, February 3, 2003.

[15] On December 28, 1937, the *Times* of London wrote, "Who can think without horror of what another widespread war would mean, waged as it would be with all the new weapons of mass destruction?" The Truman/Atlee/King Declaration of 1945 called for "the elimination from national armaments of atomic weapons and of all other major weapons adaptable to mass destruction."

of Ireland on June 23, 1985,"[16] while so-called weapons of mass destruction used in terrorist attacks (as against in war) have resulted in even more limited losses. This may be why the American Dialect Society selected *weapons of mass destruction* as its 2002 "word of the year," ratifying its status as a widely used but "long-winded phrase whose meaning reflects a nation's worry about war with Iraq."[17]

Saddam Hussein may have been trying to acquire nuclear weapons (as are many other nations, including such Middle Eastern adversaries of America as Syria and Iran), but he almost certainly had, and in the past unquestionably used, biological and chemical weapons. This was the brunt of Colin Powell's evidence presented to the U.N. Security Council in February 2003.[18] Yet the term *WMD* implies that to have and use biochemical weapons is tantamount to having and using nuclear weapons. Possessing laboratory anthrax strains (provided at least in part by the United States in the 1980s when Saddam was America's "friend" in the war against Iran)[19] is no different under the loose logic of WMD

---

[16] Mark Juergensmeyer, *Terror in the Mind of God: The Global Rise of Religious Violence* (Berkeley: University of California Press, 2002), p. 121.

[17] The American Dialect Society, founded in 1889, has been choosing a "word of the year" since 1990. See USATODAY.com, February 6, 2003.

[18] Following the American invasion of Iraq, however, little evidence was found of what in his 2003 State of the Union address President Bush had described as a vast Iraqi weapons program including "biological weapons sufficient to produce over 25,000 liters of anthrax," "more than 38,000 liters of botulinum toxin," "the materials to produce as much as 500 tons of sarin, mustard and VX nerve agent," "upwards of 30,000 munitions capable of delivering chemical agents," and "mobile biological weapons labs . . . designed to produce germ warfare agents" ("President's State of the Union Message to Congress and the Nation," *New York Times*, January 29, 2003, p. A12).

[19] The American supply house the American Type Culture Collection in Manassas, Virginia, provided the Iraqis with multiple ampoules of seventeen types of biological agents, which were used, along with French supplies, to create

than possessing thermonuclear bombs and intercontinental ballistic missiles.[20] A slippery slope, indeed, leading to dangerously wayward conclusions.

When the U.S. government incorporates biological and chemical agents into the category of WMD—perhaps in order to justify the war with Iraq or insure itself against those who might one day blame it for not giving Americans fair warning against the risks of a homeland incident—it actually magnifies the danger and enhances the fear. Terror succeeds in what it promises rather than in what it actually achieves, and so turns the effort to defend against it into its chief tool. Code the danger levels! Arrest every two-bit felon and call him a terrorist! Publicize vague threats! Label the war against it "unending"! Bring down Saddam as a WMD-addict, even if no weapons can be found! The terrorist can sit in a mountain cave or a Karachi slum and watch his enemies self-destruct around the initial fear he has seeded with a single and singular act of terror or with a few well-chosen follow-up threats that need not be made good on but which can be spread worldwide on a five-dollar tape made available to the cooperative global media. A bomb in Bali or Casablanca? The tourists stay home. An explosion in Kenya? Israelis suddenly feel as at risk abroad as they are in Tel Aviv. Some American school somewhere possibly vulnerable to an attack? Parents keep kids home or send them to school in a state of permanent anxiety. Anthrax in a television studio? American news anchors

---

biological weapons. See Philip Shenon, "Iraq Links Germs for Weapons to U.S. and France," *New York Times*, March 16, 2003, p. A18.

[20] The Department of Defense rightly includes delivery systems in its Weapons of Mass Destruction Technologies list, since absent such systems, weapons of mass destruction are of little consequence. In the DOD's words: "To be truly effective, chemical or biological agents must be spread in a diffuse cloud over a large area" (The Militarily Critical Technologies List, Office of the Under Secretary of Defense for Acquisition and Technology, Washington, D.C., February 1998).

spread their own fear to a nation of fearful viewers (scare the opinion makers and they will scare everyone else for you). And so it goes: American troops rehearsing for war in Iraq on television wearing scary space age antigas and antibacteriological gear they would never actually be required to wear and being immunized against smallpox and other toxic agents to which they were never exposed in an exercise which, though calculated to increase their combat readiness in an era of weapons of mass destruction, could only exacerbate rather than assuage their fears; government escalating the "terror level" from yellow to orange a few weeks prior to the assault on Iraq, then back to yellow with the war over, then up and back again, giving Americans no specific information but provoking quasi-hysterical behavior, including people wrapping their suburban homes in plastic sheeting, a run on duct tape (to seal off windows) and bottled water, and mothers purchasing gas masks for their two year olds. How such measures do anything other than catalyze the very fears terrorists wish to inspire is unclear. What is clear is that men who are otherwise powerless can manipulate the governments and mass media of their powerful enemies so that their adversaries do the greater part of their work for them.

In the same fashion, a single maritime attack on a tanker can raise the prospect of environmentally cataclysmic oil spills from hundreds of other ships that will never actually come under attack. The U.S. Coast Guard is now tracking several hundred "flag of convenience" cargo vessels that just might be linked to terrorism—a good thing for security, but a process that can only strike fear into the tens of millions of Americans living in America's great port cities. Fear is terrorism's tool and catalyst, the multiplier and amplifier of actual terrorist events that on the global scale are few and far between and, while devastating to those directly affected, are of less statistical consequence than say a year's traffic fatalities or the mundane tragedies of people falling off ladders at home.

President Bush declared war on terrorism and everything he has done since September 11, 2001, seems tethered to that fateful day's events. As Peter Boyer has written, in response "Rumsfeld wanted an unconventional war . . . and it would come as close as a Western nation can come to answering terrorism in kind."[21] Yet it is not terrorism but fear that is the enemy, and in the end, fear will not defeat fear. Fear's empire leaves no room for democracy, while democracy refuses to make room for fear. In free societies, Franklin Roosevelt reminded us, "The only thing we have to fear is fear itself." Free women and men engaged in governing themselves are far less vulnerable to fear than are spectators, passively watching their anxious governments try to intimidate others. Preventive war will not in the end prevent terrorism; only preventive democracy can do that.

---

[21] Peter J. Boyer, "The New War Machine," *The New Yorker*, June 30, 2003.

PART ONE

Pax Americana;
or,
Preventive War

1

Eagles and Owls

Oderint dum metuant.
(Let them hate as long as they fear.)
—*Emperor Caligula*

The course of this nation does not depend
on the decisions of others.
—*President George W. Bush, 2003*[1]

In terrorism's shadow, the United States today is torn between the temptation to reassert its natural right to independence (whether expressed as splendid isolation or unilateralist intervention) and the imperative to risk new and experimental forms of international cooperation. The desire to reassert hegemony and declare independence from the world emanates from hubris laced with fear; it aims at coercing the world to join America—"you're with us or you're with the terrorists!" Call the goal of this desire *Pax Americana*, a universal peace imposed by American arms: fear's empire founded in right's good name, because it matters not if they hate us as long as they fear us. Pax Americana, like the imperial Roman hegemony (Pax Romana) on which it models itself, envisions global comity imposed on the world by unilateral American

[1] State of the Union Address, January 28, 2003.

military force—with as much cooperation and law as does not stand in the way of unilateral decision making and action.

The imperative to risk innovation and forge cooperation, to seek an alternative to Pax Americana, arises out of realism: it issues in strategies aimed at allowing America to join the world. Call this alternative *lex humana*, universal law rooted in human commonality. Call it preventive democracy. Lex humana works for global comity within the framework of universal rights and law, conferred by multilateral political, economic, and cultural cooperation—with only as much common military action as can be authorized by common legal authority, whether in the Congress, in multilateral treaties, or through the United Nations.

Pax Americana reasserts American sovereignty, if necessary over the entire planet; lex humana seeks a pooling of sovereignties (Europe is one example) around international law and institutions, recognizing that interdependence has already rendered sovereignty's national frontiers porous and its powers ever less sufficient. Following successful military campaigns in Afghanistan and Iraq (and before them, in Yugoslavia), the Pax Americana strategy would appear to have the upper hand. But history suggests that American policy is cyclic, and interdependence argues (as will I) that lex humana is the better long-term strategy.

In its diplomatic history, America has pursued both foreign policy on horseback (The "Lone Ranger" approach typified by Teddy Roosevelt) and a "Concert of Nations" approach stressing multilateral cooperation. Since 9/11 at least, the Bush administration (as well as both congressional political parties and a great number of Americans) have seemed to veer ambivalently between the two—approaching the Iraq question, for example, with a dizzying ambivalence that left America as a unilateralist scourge of international law, multilateralism, and the United Nations on Mondays, Wednesdays, and Fridays and their multilateralist savior on Tuesdays, Thursdays, and Saturdays. Just a few weeks before the American war on Iraq began, polls suggested nearly two-thirds of the American public supported a war only if it was fought with the approval of the United Nations. A couple of weeks into the campaign, two-thirds approved of war without U.N. support.

For all of President Bush's fervent unilateralist conviction, the country, and to some degree even Bush's own administration, is divided into antagonistic camps of what I will call not hawks and chickens (or chickenhawks and doves) but eagles and owls. The eagle is a patriotic predator of a particular kind—one, in my metaphor, that takes its prey at midday without much forethought. The owl, though it too is a hunter, is keen-sighted even in a world of shadows and farseeing even at night. Like Hegel's celebrated Owl of Minerva, it takes flight only at dusk, when it can see the shape of things at the end of the day. The eagles inside the Bush administration include obvious members of the war party such as Vice-President Richard Cheney and Secretary of Defense Donald Rumsfeld, but many others too, including Deputy Secretary of Defense Paul Wolfowitz, former Pentagon Defense Policy Board chairman Richard Perle, and Undersecretary of State John Bolton. The owls include not only Secretary of State Colin Powell but the Joint Chiefs of State as well as much of the traditional foreign policy establishment and career officials at the State and Defense Departments.

When the President heeds the cautioning voices of owlish insiders like former chairman of the Joint Chiefs and Secretary of State Colin Powell or owlish outsiders like Generals Anthony Zinni and Brent Scowcroft, the eagles can be cajoled into multilateralist cooperation. But they are preternaturally impatient. They are fixed on the sovereign right of an independent United States and of its "chosen people" to defend itself where, when, and how it chooses against enemies it alone has the right to identify and define. Far from clinging blindly to sovereignty, they know the clock is running out on its prerogatives and so they seek to impose America precipitously on the world by all means available including military threats, assassination, and preemptive and preventive war, along with traditional multilateral deterrence and containment. They know what fear can do to America and seek instead to make it America's weapon.

The Iraq war was a leading example of the eagles' militancy, but their new strategic doctrine has consequences that go far beyond Iraq. Whatever else it may be called, the Iraq strategy was no one-time adventure predicated on "wag the dog" styles of reasoning. Saddam did not suddenly become our mortal adversary because of oil, because of Israel, because the president wished to avenge his father, because the Republican Party knew how a war would play in diverting attention from the declining economy in the fall '02 elections and beyond. Rather, the administration's approach to Saddam Hussein (whose power and so-called weapons of mass destruction previous American administrations helped to secure) was present as a concept well before 9/11 and is rooted in a deep and abiding conception of America's world as a place of danger for Americans.[2]

The new strategy predicts war unending: where intimidation (fear's first option) fails, a succession of armed interventions in country after country after country, from Iraq's axis of evil partners in Iran and North Korea to countries where shadowy terrorist relationships are intimated, from Syria and Somalia to Indonesia and the Philippines—to which the United States committed a thousand men including three hundred combat soldiers in February 2003. It

---

[2] "Before the [September 11] attacks, the Pentagon had been working for months on developing a military option for Iraq," reports Bob Woodward. At a meeting just a few days after 9/11, "Rumsfeld was raising the possibility that they could take advantage of the opportunity offered by the terrorist attacks to go after Saddam immediately" (Woodward, *Bush at War*, p. 49).

predicts picking off adversaries wherever they are found, whether
in hostile regimes or among friends and allies with terrorist associations such as Egypt, Saudi Arabia, and Pakistan. It predicts
strikes—even "sledgehammer" tactical nuclear strikes—against
nuclear powers including countries with million-man armies like
North Korea.[3] In short, it predicts a war made permanent by a perverse strategy that targets inappropriate but visible national
stand-ins (rogue states and evil regimes, for example) in place of
appropriate but invisible terrorist enemies.

The administration's most forceful eagle is neither Vice-
President Dick Cheney nor Defense Secretary Donald Rumsfeld,
nor the far right wing of the Republican Party, but President Bush
himself, a man motivated by an overriding belief in the potency of
missionary rationales for and military solutions to the challenges of
global insecurity. President Bush has said over and over again since
9/11 that his presidential mandate is defined in his own mind
almost exclusively by the war for American security in a perilous
world. He has defined that war in terms of a vision of exceptional
American virtue and a countervision of foreign malevolence that
may strike outsiders as self-righteous and even Manichaean (divid-
ing the world into camps of the good and the evil) but which is
powerfully motivating within the United States and which gives to
his policies an uncompromising militancy invulnerable to world
public opinion.

---

[3] In an op-ed essay laced with fear and entitled "Secret, Scary Plans," *New
York Times* editorial writer Nicholas D. Kristof writes that the United States is
developing contingency plans for "surgical cruise missile strikes" or even a
"sledgehammer bombing," including the use of tactical nuclear weapons
against North Korean nuclear facilities. Kristof notes that neither South Korea
nor Japan understand "the gravity of the situation . . . partly because they do
not think this administration would be crazy enough to consider a military
strike against North Korea." Kristof concludes: "They're wrong" (*New York
Times*, February 28, 2003, p. A25).

In the epoch-defining speech he gave at the National Cathedral a few days after 9/11, the president said: "We are here in the middle hour of our grief. But our responsibility to history is already clear: to answer these attacks and rid the world of evil." At the conclusion of his speech, as Bob Woodward describes it in his semi-hagiographic account *Bush at War*, the congregation "stood and sang 'The Battle Hymn of the Republic.' " Whether the president "was casting his mission and that of the country in the grand vision of God's master plan,"[4] as Woodward has it, or merely deploying a familiar American moralism, his religious rhetoric has been galvanizing both to his backers and his adversaries. The "axis of evil" phrase was as productive within the United States as it was counterproductive in the rest of the world.[5] Where others feared an unprovoked war, President Bush saw a wholly provoked campaign against "evil ones," a campaign in the name of liberty: "either you believe in freedom and want to—and worry about the human condition, or you don't."[6]

When President Bush was told by CIA Director George Tenet that if he really wanted to take on the countries that supported or harbored terrorists, he'd be facing a "sixty country problem," the president replied "we'll pick them off one at a time"[7]—Pax Americana by gradualist means. This has turned out to be crucial to the

[4] Woodward, *Bush at War*, p. 67.

[5] President Bush first used the phrase in his January 29, 2002, State of the Union speech: "States like these," he said, naming Iraq, Iran, and North Korea, "and their terrorist allies, constitute an axis of evil, arming to threaten the peace of the world."

[6] Quoted by Patrick E. Tyler, "A Signal Moment Ahead," *New York Times*, December 8, 2002, p. A30. Citing the interview with Bob Woodward from which the comment was taken, Tyler remarks wisely: "Those comments suggest that Mr. Bush is not engaged in an opportunistic whipping up of an Iraq crisis, as some of his critics allege, as a way to divert the country from a troubled economy."

[7] Cited by Woodward, *Bush at War*, p. 33.

Bush administration's implementation of its new national security doctrine and should give pause to those who believe Iraq is a special case of no predictive value for future American strategy. In truth, the Bush administration has refused to be drawn into a new struggle until it has "picked off" its current adversary. Pressing as Iraq was, it was only a year after 9/11 and well after the military phase of the Taliban campaign was concluded that Saddam Hussein became America's primary obsession. During the Iraq phase, North Korea was shoved to the side, even when doing so made America's policy seem incoherent and hypocritical. But impatient eagles were already developing their contingency plans for Korea and perhaps Iran and Syria as well,[8] and they were undertaking contingency planning for more remote theaters of possible terrorist war in places like Indonesia and the Philippines. "One at a time" suggests a deeper coherence to what otherwise seems a jumbled set of competing initiatives. It suggests that the Iraq war was not a special case but part of a preventive war plan whose compass was and is the world.

The eagles are unilateralists with attitude, because their self-righteous wrath is steeped in the lore of American exceptionalism. Believing the United States is unique allows hawkishness to roost in virtue, uses innocence to excuse righteous war, and employs sovereign independence to rationalize strategic unilateralism. Thus, in rationalizing the war in Iraq after it was over, President Bush told Coast Guard graduates:

> Because America loves peace. America will always work and sacrifice for the expansion of freedom. The advance of freedom is more than an interest we pursue. It is a calling we follow. . . . As

---

[8] George Tenet testified to Congress on February 11, 2003, that there are "disturbing signs that al Qaeda has established a presence in both Iran and Iraq." By the same token, Undersecretary of State John Bolton told Israeli officials that after defeating Iraq, the United States would "deal with" Iran, Syria, and North Korea (Paul Krugman, "Things to Come," *New York Times*, March 18, 2003, p. A33).

a people dedicated to civil rights, we are driven to define the human rights of others. We are the nation that liberated continents and concentration camps. We are the nation of the Marshall Plan, the Berlin Airlift and the Peace Corps. We are the nation that ended the oppression of Afghan women, and we are the nation that closed the torture chambers of Iraq. . . . America seeks to expand, not the borders of our country, but the realm of liberty.[9]

The anxious owls, seers of the new interdependence, insist that neither safety nor liberty can any longer be secured by even the most powerful of nations if it operates alone and relies exclusively on sovereign military might. However much they prize sovereignty, the owls believe its essence was compromised long before the attacks of 9/11. However much they understand the uses of force, they know its ends must be in conformity with law if its true purposes are to be served. However much they appreciate fear's hold over men, they know that its power can be used by both terrorists and legitimate states while democracy's influence belongs to democratic societies alone. And so they pursue diplomacy, cooperation, democratization, and collective security not because they are dovish but because they are realist. At President Bush's war cabinet meetings, Colin Powell was as fierce in his militancy as anyone after the 9/11 attacks: "This is not just an attack against America, this is an attack against civilization," he proclaimed. "This is a long war and a war we have to win." But he spoke as an owl, and added a note of prudence: "We are engaging with the world. We want to make this a long-standing coalition."[10] As wisely as the owls sometimes can speak about the new world of interdependence, they are

[9] George W. Bush, "Remarks by the President in Commencement Address to United States Coast Guard Academy," New London, Conn., May 21, 2003.

[10] Cited by Woodward, *Bush at War*, p. 65. Powell made forty-seven telephone calls to world leaders in the first few days after 9/11, while the eagles were screaming for war.

not always clearly heard in the clamor of patriotic eagles calling for the vindication of sovereign independence and a rule of fear advanced by strategies of shock and awe. When Secretary of Defense Rumsfeld and his assistant Paul Wolfowitz started campaigning for an assault on Iraq before the war against the Taliban was even in the planning stage, Powell said to the chairman of the Joint Chiefs of Staff, "What the hell, what are these guys thinking about? Can't you get these guys back in the box?"[11]

The eagles' impatience sometimes outruns the "one at a time" corollary to the preventive war doctrine; for the eagles have sharp, if limited, vision and cannot easily be put back in "the box." They too may recognize the reality of interdependence, but they regard it with skepticism, being no longer the tough-minded realists of the Cold War years when the delicate balance of nuclear terror dictated prudence and patience: to contain rather than to interdict, to deter aggressive acts rather than to transform aggressive regimes. They have become the new idealists—idealists of unilateralism, and war—believing hegemonic power gives them the means to strike quickly and decisively. In their romantic enthusiasm, they are absolutely certain they can overwhelm interdependence through acts of sovereign self-assertion, override global complexity with nationalist daring, liberate people in bondage by bombing them into submission, democratize women and men who have never known freedom by executing their rulers.

Surprisingly, it is the owls—aging old birds, strategic toughs, and wary veterans—who are the new realists. To them interdependence is less an aspiration, the world as they wish it were, than a

---

[11] Ibid., p. 61. By the onset of the Iraq war in March 2003, Colin Powell was himself out of the box, speaking with the eagles against the machinations of the French and their supporters at the United Nations. One may surmise, however, that having lost the struggle to prevent the intervention in Iraq, Powell was keeping his counsel for another day, hoping to be able to play the diplomatic card again after the war.

pressing reality that mandates working with others through the law because that is the only way interdependence can be survived. They are not awed by fear, whether they use it or experience it used against them. They are less convinced of its efficacy than Machiavelli once was, perhaps because they understand that terrorists live beyond fear's empire, in a place where death is preferred to life and being dispatched by America's hegemonic military machine is a badge of honor.

Preoccupied with enforcement and persuaded (rightly) that law is meaningless in the absence of enforcement, the eagles privilege a muscular national sovereignty over treaty making and multilateral cooperation. They hope to rescue independence from the claims of interdependence by acts of sheer will punctuated by deeds of awesome power. When Secretary of State Powell warned President Bush that the coalition which supported his war against al-Qaeda might fall apart if he went after other terrorist groups or states like Iraq, the president—his eagle's eye gleaming—replied that he was unwilling to be dictated to by other countries: "At some point we may be the only ones left. That's okay with me. We are America."[12] When urged by allies to secure a second United Nations resolution to move against Iraq, he reminded them that America needed no nation's permission to defend itself. In the revealing words of an unnamed Bush administration official on the day the Iraqi government submitted its report on weapons to the United Nations at the end of 2002, the United States would not be bound by that report or the UN's reaction to it: the Iraq problem is not playing out in "a court of law," he said, "this is a matter for national security."[13]

The owls worry that the focus on enforcement will undermine the law it is supposed to strengthen. Just as overzealous cops in the

[12] Ibid., p. 81.

[13] Quoted in John F. Burns and David E. Sanger, "Iraq Says Report to the U.N. Shows No Banned Arms," *New York Times*, December 8, 2002, p. A28.

inner city can undermine the law in whose name they swing their clubs, immoderate displays of American military power sap the very notion of the law in whose name that power is being invoked. Iraq's national museum fell victim neither to Saddam nor the war that vanquished him but to the anarchy in which that war issued on the way (maybe) to democracy. Fear is a great motivator but its achievements are mostly negative. As Edmund Burke said of the terrorist sanctions by which the Jacobins tried to impose their religion of reason on France in 1789, "in the groves of their academy, at the end of every vista, you see nothing but the gallows."[14] The revolution made by the guillotine turned out to be a poor substitute for democracy.

The owls would prefer to rely on a muscular global law secured by cooperation and global governance, on enforced collective security measures rather than unilateral American might. Bob Woodward, "imagining" what Powell is thinking (this is Woodward's "method") after President Bush tells Powell he's ready to go it alone, has Powell muse, "going it alone was precisely what he (Powell) wanted to avoid if possible. He thought that the President's formulation was not realistic. Without partners, the United States could not launch an effective war even in Afghanistan, certainly not worldwide . . . tough talk might be necessary, but it should not be confused with policy."[15] Fear may elicit silence, even submission; it rarely produces lasting security.

Neither eagles nor owls lack conviction, and both possess compelling arguments. The eagles and owls within the Bush administration have even managed a degree of collaboration that has achieved some remarkable successes, making the obvious evident: power and law need each other if democratic outcomes are to be secured. But the eagles, left to themselves (which is where finally they want to be left) are wrong. Indeed, by virtue of their excep-

---

[14] Edmund Burke, *Reflections on the Revolution in France*, Everyman Edition (New York: E. P. Dutton, 1910), p. 75.

[15] Woodward, *Bush at War*, p. 81.

tionalist idealism, which puts them on the wrong side of history, they are wrong disastrously. The preventive war doctrine that is their signature strategy, although it has won bold short-term victories, is potentially catastrophic for America as well as for the world.

The owls are right, if only by dint of their new realism, a realism that recognizes that history can never again be on America's side unless America is on the side of interdependence. It is not that law can manage without enforcement or that governance is possible without power. The important policy differences ultimately turn on whether power is guided by and conforms to law or aims simply to subdue, pacify, and dominate. In preventive war, it does not, and although the owls inside the administration have not said so explicitly, a realist and effective national security policy and preventive war are fundamentally incompatible.

What is compelling to the eagles (and in this they are right) is that the unrivaled global dominion of American military, economic, and cultural power means there can be no viable world without America: no prosperity for the poor, no rule of law for nations, no justice for peoples, no peace for humankind. Yet what is compelling for the owls (they too are right) is that American hegemony stands challenged by the ineluctable reality of interdependence—a reality signaled by the vulnerability of the most independent and powerful states in the face of globalization. That is to say, by the internationalization of jobs, production, financial capital, and consumption; by the transnational character of public health plagues like AIDS, SARS, and the West Nile virus; by transregional ecological threats like global warming and species extinction; by the globalization of information technology; and by the spread of nonstate-based systems of crime and terrorism. What this means is that there can be no viable America without the world: no safety for American civilians, no security for American investors, no liberty for American citizens, unless there is safety, security, and liberty for all.

2

The Myth of Independence

Our calling as a blessed country is to make the world better.
—*President George W. Bush, 2003*[1]

I never knew a man who had better motives
for all the trouble he caused.
—*Graham Greene,* The Quiet American

A nation creates its past no less than its future. The myths we conceive to account for our national origins, character, and destiny may seem rooted in history, but history itself has a fabulist dimension whose objective is the invention of roots.[2] From its founding, America regarded itself as unique and hence exempt from the laws that otherwise govern the life and destiny of other nations. James Madison insisted that while "democracies have ever been spectacles of turbulence and contention; have ever been

---

[1] State of the Union Address, January 28, 2003.

[2] I use the term *myth* as Richard Slotkin does when he notes that "myth expresses ideology in a narrative, its language is metaphorical and suggestive rather than logical and analytical." What he calls "mythic icons" offer "a poetic construction of tremendous economy and compression" evoking "an implicit understanding of the entire historical scenario" (*Gunfighter Nation: The Myth of the Frontier in Twentieth-Century America* [Norman: Oklahoma University Press, 1998], p. 6).

found incompatible with personal security or the rights of property," the new American experiment in republicanism "opens a different prospect, and promises the cure for which we are seeking."[3] Thomas Jefferson, the architect (among other things) of a "greater" continental America via the Louisiana Purchase and the Lewis and Clark expedition to the great Northwest, noted that the American experience offered "a new proof of the falsehood of Montesquieu's doctrine, that a republic can be preserved in only a small territory. The reverse is the truth. Had our territory been even a third only of what it is, we were gone."[4] America's novelty is what makes it so fascinating a subject to Alexis de Tocqueville, who speaks of the young nation's "unbounded imagination" that "grows and dilates beyond all measure." The "magnificent image" Americans have of themselves "does not meet the gaze of Americans at intervals only; it may be said to haunt every one of them in his least as well as his most important actions and to be always flitting before his mind."[5]

America is not exceptional in its exceptionalist biases of course: the Swiss speak of *Sonderfall Schweiz* (the special Swiss case), France long understood itself as having had a unique civilizing mission (*mission civilatrice*) linked to its commitment to liberty, equality, and fraternity (it retains more than a residue of this today), while societies from ancient Athens to classical China have boasted of their uniqueness by deeming all others "barbarians." Even lib-

[3] James Madison, Federalist Number 10, *The Federalist Papers*, Modern Library Edition (New York: Random House, 1937), pp. 58–59.

[4] Cited by Walter LaFeber, *The American Age: U.S. Foreign Policy at Home and Abroad, 1750 to the Present*, 2nd ed. (New York: W. W. Norton, 1994), p. 52. Montesquieu's *Spirit of the Laws* was a *locus classicus* for republican theory and for the claim that republics could not maintain their liberty when their territory became extensive and hence necessarily "imperial."

[5] Alexis de Tocqueville, *Democracy in America*, vol. 2, ed. Phillips Bradley (New York: Vintage Books, 1990), bk. 1, chap. 17, p. 74.

eral Jews have imagined an exceptionalist Germany. Holocaust diarist Victor Klemperer wrote, "We, we Germans are better than other nations. Freer in thought, purer in feeling, juster in action. We, we Germans, are truly a chosen people."[6] No nation, however, has been so committed to its exceptionalist myths in its policies and practices as the United States, and none have made exceptionalism so central to their national life and their international politics. Among the exceptionalist myths that fire the American imagination, the myth of innocence is perhaps paramount—buttressed by the ideology of independence.

Herman Melville explores it about as well as any American, but it is evident in the writings of Walt Whitman and Henry James after Melville, and evident in the Puritans and the American founders before him.[7] At the time of the founding, Europeans already looked to America as a second Eden, a new land beckoning a chosen people. Tom Paine had cast the myth of innocent beginnings as the basis for a revolution that would look not forward but back to recapture the ancient rights and liberties of Englishmen. America, being a place where men (in Paine's phrase) might "start the world over again," allowed Americans to look back and restart the human story as if "in the beginning of time."[8] Jefferson's Declaration of Independence recalled rights more natural and ancient than any

[6] Cited by Jason Epstein, "Leviathan," *New York Review of Books*, May 1, 2003.

[7] For an account of Melville's role in portraying the myth of American innocence see my "Melville and the Myth of American Innocence," in *Aspects of Melville*, ed. David Scribner (Pittsfield, Mass.: Berkshire County Historical Society at Arrowhead, 2001).

[8] "The case and circumstances of America present themselves as in the beginning of the world . . . we are brought at once to the point of seeing government begin, as if we had lived in the beginning of time" (Thomas Paine, *The Rights of Man*, in *Complete Works*, vol. 1 [New York: Citadel Press, 1945], p. 376).

political bonds, rights that justified the overthrow of an abusive regime and allowed men to "assume among the Powers of the Earth, the separate and equal Station to which the Laws of Nature and Nature's God entitle them." Legitimacy itself acquired in America the ring of innocence, for illegitimacy was always regarded as the child of wayward history and corruption, of rights abused and set aside, while legitimacy was a product of a people's fresh and natural "duty to throw off [abusive] Government, and provide new Guards for their future Security."

During the Enlightenment, America appeared to many Europeans as an escape from Europe's freighted history. Gazing on the European narrative of intolerance, religious war, persecution, and fratricide, Voltaire had called history little more than a record of mankind's errors and follies. How different America seemed. Because the New World was "empty" (the red man was invisible in Europe's eyes, part of the continent's flora and fauna), it was quite literally a tabula rasa, a blank tablet upon which new men might inscribe a new history.

It was this virgin America John Locke must have had in mind when he wrote in his *Second Treatise of Civil Government* that those discontent with the constraints of an oppressive social contract, if revolution was impossible, could repair instead to the "empty places" (*loci vacuii*) of the world and start society over again. Crèvecoeur's widely read and justly famous *Letters from an American Farmer*, written in the period between the Revolution and the making of the Constitution, imagined in the American a "new man," and in America itself what Crèvecoeur described as a great "asylum . . . [where] everything tended to regenerate [Americans]: new laws, a new mode of living, a new social system."[9] One

---

[9] J. Hector St. John de Crèvecoeur, *Letters from an American Farmer* (New York: Penguin, 1981), pp. 68–69.

can already imagine the hubris with which a nation that conceived of itself in these terms might one day project itself abroad. Yet Crèvecoeur himself adumbrated America's founding attachment to the rule of law: in posing the question "by what power" such a "surprising metamorphosis" might have been performed, he answered "by that of the laws."

While the European political passions from which America's founders had fled were drenched in religion, America's ardent new civil religion nestled in the orderly bosom of a written constitution in which were inscribed the inalterable laws of nature. America's patriotism was rooted in ideas not blood, in law not kinship, in voluntary citizenship not ascriptive roots, in constitutional faith not confessional orthodoxy. Despite Madison's focus on the plays of interests in the Federalist Papers, America's foreign policy began with the presumption of American virtue and consequently with an inclination to avoid "entangling foreign alliances" as well as to insulate the hemisphere from foreign encroachment (what would in time become the Monroe Doctrine).

Whether in the name of interest or virtue, the newness of the American experiment led James Madison to insist on the need for a new experimental science to draw up a constitution for this country unlike any for which Europe's traditional constitutionalist political theory might have been pertinent. Alexis de Tocqueville recognized in the Jacksonian republic he toured in the early 1830s an entirely new episode in the young history of democracy. The American mythology mixed a deep respect for the law with fresh energy and untutored naïveté: a lex humana made fresh and palpable by what Americans regarded as the preternatural innocence of their claim on liberty secured by law. It was as if the hypothetical innocence of Rousseau's state of nature had been written into America's actual beginnings. Even after the blood lessons of a terrible civil war, innocence counted among Walt Whitman's most touching themes. Slavery and the battle against it notwithstanding, America retained the glow of a virtuous innocence right through the Gilded Age heading into the new century, when Henry James could ponder the persistent foolishness of American "innocents abroad" and revel in the adventures of the likes of the ever fresh naïf Daisy Miller.

How was such a fresh and innocent nation to conduct itself abroad? How to survive in a world of nations steeped in crime and folly? These were questions that begged America's other predilection for pragmatism and adaptation (these too would mark and perhaps rescue American foreign policy from some of the less happy consequences of American myth). They were deep enough to trouble American literati as well as American statesmen—none more than Herman Melville. Melville's stuttering foretopman in his novella *Billy Budd, Sailor* made for an ambivalent example.[10] He was so like young America: a foundling, a happy illiterate who lacked completely the "wisdom of the serpent." If America was a new Eden reclaimed from Europe's sullied past, Billy promised something of what that new Eden's Adam might be: "little more than a sort of upright barbarian, much such perhaps as Adam presumably might have been ere the urbane Serpent wriggled himself into his company." Billy Budd facing his tormentor Claggart could be seen as America confronting the Europe from which its founders had escaped, "a young horse fresh from the pasture suddenly inhaling a vile whiff from some chemical factory." But Billy ends up the victim of his enraged innocence, the intemperate blow he strikes in the name of good intentions condemning him to execution. A foreign policy calls for more than the rage of the wronged.

---

[10] Readers will recall that Melville's Billy, rendered mute by rage at the evil and duplicitous Claggart's mischief, strikes out righteously at him with a killing blow—leading the ship's captain to condemn Billy reluctantly to death for his understandable but nonetheless capital "crime."

What is only implicit in *Billy Budd* becomes explicit in Melville's "Benito Cereno." The American protagonist of "Benito Cereno" is Amasa Delano, captain of a whaling ship. His confrontation with nefarious foreigners on a ship of deceit that is not only a slaver but a slaver in the midst of a righteous but awful mutiny, resonates with American piety: the incomprehension of the virtuous in the face of deep villainy. For though he is a far more reflective and temperate character than Budd, Captain Delano embodies even more than Billy, an American innocence so opaque in the face of evil that it seems equally insensible to slavery and the rebellion against slavery.[11]

Although Melville does not explicitly acknowledge it, what is remarkable in Captain Delano's blindness to evil is his incapacity to recognize the moral debacle of slavery itself. How maddening his reaction must seem to those who know enough of men to understand both the impulse to bondage and the impulse to be freed from it—maddening in a fashion akin perhaps to how much of the Third World today reacts to America's claims to moral righteousness and governmental superiority; maddening in the way Alden Pyle in Graham Greene's *Quiet American* is infuriating to the Vietnamese he blithely plans to liberate from both the French and their own culture.

What exercises the self-assured Delano is the slaves' mutiny, rather than their status as a human cargo being delivered into New

[11] In "Benito Cereno," Delano intercepts a Spanish slaver on its way to the New World on which the cargo, so to say, has taken the crew captive. When boarded by Delano's party, the lead rebel, a bold and literate figure who is in fact in charge following a successful mutiny, pretends to be subservient to the Spanish captain. So impenetrable is Delano's American innocence that he cannot fathom what is unfolding so clearly before him. He takes what is a relationship of treachery and dissemblance to be a "spectacle of fidelity, on the one hand, and confidence on the other." Delano, Melville writes, is a "person of a singularly undistrustful good nature, not liable . . . to indulge in personal alarms, any way involving the imputation of malign evil in man." Like Billy Budd, he can scarcely comprehend evil even when he looks deep into its eyes.

World servitude. Melville forgives the Yankee Captain (as the slaves on board the slaver presumably cannot), in the face of "machinations and deceptions" he cannot fathom, for not being able to judge "the conduct of one with the recesses of whose condition he is not acquainted." These are more the recesses of slavery's ignominy than of the slave revolt, however—recesses whose inaccessibility to the American imagination (before Lincoln set the record straight at Gettysburg) permitted America to rue the Civil War more than the slavery that was at its heart. So then did Captain Delano seem to rue the mutiny by the slaves more than their bondage—though he intuitively understood there was some connection between the two. Melville discloses (and not for the last time) that fatal hypocrisy with which Americans presumptuously celebrate a putative virtue that in fact disguises moral blindness and hence looks to others like cynicism, if not wickedness.

Captain Delano becomes the perfect emblem of American innocence: the hypocrite-innocent, oblivious not only to the hoary corruptions of foreign lands staggering under the burdens of despotic histories but to the evils residing within America's own heart (it is for America's slave culture that the slave ship is bound)—certain only that evil is foreign, virtue American. For Delano, the securing of the blessings of liberty requires not an internal cleansing but a warding off of external enemies.

The myth of innocence captured by Melville has persisted down into and through the twentieth century and right into this new millennium, where it colors and helps explain the Bush administration's new preventive war doctrine. In much of the nineteenth century and the first third of the twentieth, it spawned an isolationist foreign policy that made America reluctant to enter Europe's corrupt wars until forced to do so—reluctantly in World War I, and only by dint of a treacherous enemy surprise attack in World

War II.[12] Yet this isolationism was and is about more than just chauvinism or narrow self-interest. It represented the conviction that to stay pure, America had to steer clear of foreign involvements; that its foreign policy could not follow base interests as Europe's had always supposedly done, but had to be conducted in the name of all-American values such as democracy, liberty, and piety.

In his classic lecture "Politics as a Vocation," the great German social thinker Max Weber offered a comfortless portrait of the real world of politics: "the world is governed by demons and he who lets himself in for politics . . . contracts with diabolical powers." Americans living in what they regarded as a second Eden really seemed to believe the only way to deflect the terror of these demons was to ward off the world, to stay out of its compromising and blood-drenched politics. When in tune with the once dominant geography of the United States and with the distinctive interests of Europe and America, these sturdy myths of independence and innocence served American growth and development well for several centuries.

Yet in a world where the oceans are as puddles and sovereign national frontiers so many archaic markings on old maps, the daily realities of interdependence everywhere contradict the idea of sovereign autonomy. They insist that attention be paid to the claims of others. They render an obsession with piety and virtue wrapped in a blanket of sovereign independence not just irrelevant but corrosive to the need and capacity to make tough choices between competing evils. The paradox is that an America that believes itself so innocent that it must be saved from the rest of the world by assuming a fearful solitude—or transform that world by imposing a fear-

---

[12] So dependent on provocation was American involvement in Europe's wars that the absurd claim Roosevelt had staged Pearl Harbor (by ignoring warnings) had a certain lunatic currency among those deeply committed to isolationism.

some hegemony over it—puts not only that world but itself at grave risk. This is perhaps why America's toughest critic today is Europe, which learned the lessons of interdependence the hard way through two world wars that destroyed not only the nationalist hubris of its member states but the very meaning of their prized sovereignty. Robert Kagan suggests that Europe resists the drawing of the mighty American sword because it has lost its will and its courage, and is playing a foolish, feminine Venus to America's truculent Mars.[13] *New York Times* op-ed writer Tom Friedman, growing tired of the wary, nettlesome European voice he once liked to translate for irked Americans, now agrees with Kagan, pointing to a "yawning power gap" that is producing "all sorts of resentment, insecurities and diverging attitudes as to what constitutes the legitimate exercise of force."[14] Aside from the fact that calling Germany weak and peace-minded might seem to most readers of European history to be the highest compliment one could pay it, Germany and the Europeans have learned the hard way that war never brings collective security and that preening hegemons, even when they preach peace and virtue, perhaps especially when they preach peace and virtue, are themselves likely to be the greatest peril peace faces. Hence, it comes as no surprise that in a *Time* magazine poll (wholly unscientific) conducted in January 2003 asking Europeans which nations posed the greatest risk to peace, Iraq and North Korea scored around 7–8 percent each while the United States polled a startling 80 percent.[15]

[13] Robert Kagan, *Of Paradise and Power: America and Europe in the New World Order* (New York, Alfred A. Knopf, 2003).

[14] Thomas L. Friedman, "Ah, Those Principled Europeans," *New York Times*, February 2, 2003, sec. 4, p. 15.

[15] *Time Europe*, February 6, 2003. *Time* noted that theirs was "an unscientific, informal survey for the interest and enjoyment of Time.com users and may not be indicative of popular opinion." Other polls confirm the *Time* results, however.

American exceptionalism has from the start given to American foreign policy an idealist character. As critics like theorist Hans Morgenthau and practitioners such as George Kennan and Henry Kissinger have endlessly pointed out, this idealism has been foreign policy's most troublesome feature. Yet for all the carping by realists, America has been sure of its uniqueness, and few presidents have eschewed the public resonance of American virtue in rationalizing their international strategies whether in war or peace. Recent critics of President Bush's religiosity and "born again" convictions seem to have overlooked this exceptionalist history.[16]

From its early adventures in Mexico before the Civil War (which Abraham Lincoln opposed as a congressman and which some Republicans regarded as a Southern Democratic ploy to extend slavery) right through to Vietnam, America has always managed to find idealistic reasons to justify interventions that could not be tied to self-defense and that realists considered the product of self-interest and ambition. This was true in Cuba and the U.S.-led campaign to "free" the Philippines from Spain (1898), in Mexico (1914), in Haiti (1915), in the Dominican Republic (1916 and again in 1965), and in Grenada (1983). The reasons emanated from America's exceptionalist virtues—its will to extend the compass of liberty, to bring free markets to its trading partners, to bring democracy to the whole wide world.

William James saw in exceptionalism's claims a fateful if not always fatal hypocrisy: "We had supposed ourselves (with all our crudity and barbarity in certain ways) a better nation morally than the rest, safe at home, and without the old savage ambition, destined to exert great international influence by throwing in our

---

[16] See, for example, the *Newsweek* cover story, "Bush and God," March 10, 2003, or "God and American Diplomacy," *The Economist*, February 6, 2003. Jimmy Carter was actually the first "born again" president.

'moral weight.' . . . Dreams! Human nature is everywhere the same; and at least temptation all the old military passions rise, and sweep everything before them."[17]

The references to American's own goodwill and preternatural innocence put its motives not only beyond interest but beyond scrutiny. The rationales drip with an easy virtue, again and again and again: "We went down to Mexico," proclaimed President Wilson, "to make it safe for democracy." World War I, as well as the League of Nations, would have the same aim. That mother of modern wars was also the war that would put an end to war. World War II avenged Pearl Harbor and liberated Europe and Asia from an earlier and more powerful "evil axis." Vietnam drew America in, as Presidents Kennedy, Johnson, and Nixon all agreed, because it was a potential Southeast Asian domino that, if it fell, would be followed by other neighboring nations, opening the way for the triumph of totalitarian communism. (As a rationale for intervention, the appeal to falling dominos edged toward preventive war thinking.) The Cold War was a long-term holding operation against an "evil empire."

Like American realists, foreign skeptics see behind every idealist expression or reference to Divine Providence some covert interest: in the Monroe Doctrine ("Europe, stay out of our backyard!"), an excuse for a hemispheric American empire; in isolationism ("no entangling foreign alliances!"), a wish to be exempt from the heavy costs of commitments and treaties; and in "democratic interventionism" of the kind that rationalized the American push under

---

[17] William James, in a quote reprinted in *The Nation*, December 23, 2002. Realist criticisms of moralizing in foreign policy have been offered by theorists like Lord Acton ("a nation has neither permanent friends nor permanent enemies, only permanent interests"), Henry Morgenthau, E. H. Carr, and George Kennan, inter alios.

McKinley and Teddy Roosevelt[18] for empire in the Caribbean and the Pacific, and animated Woodrow Wilson's involvements in Mexico and in Europe ("make the world safe for democracy!"), a rationale for global ambitions. But most Americans, moved by exceptionalism, understood these same doctrines—whether they counseled a fortress America that stayed home or an aggressive America that straddled the globe—as rooted in virtue and justified by America's core "decency" and commitment to liberal democracy. In the midst of his campaign to persuade both Americans and the United Nations to embark on war against Iraq, President Bush thus reminded all who would listen that "America is the greatest nation, full of the most decent people, on the face of the earth."[19]

Moralizing may satisfy America's exceptionalist expectations. President Bush drew little criticism for saying at West Point, "Some worry that it is somehow undiplomatic or impolite to speak the language of right and wrong. I disagree. Different circumstances require different methods, but not different moralities."[20] The trouble is, the language of moral absolutism makes negotiated solutions to international conflict nearly impossible.

President Bush's moralizing rhetoric of good and evil in the cam-

---

[18] "Chronic wrongdoing . . . may in America, as elsewhere, ultimately require intervention by some civilized nation, and in the Western Hemisphere the adherence of the United States to the Monroe Doctrine may lead the United States, however reluctantly, in flagrant cases of such wrongdoing or impotence, to the exercise of an international police power" (President Theodore Roosevelt, "The Roosevelt Corollary to the Monroe Doctrine," 1904).

[19] Cited by David E. Sanger, ""Bush Juggles the Roles of Leader and Cheerleader," *New York Times*, October 28, 2002, p. A15.

[20] George W. Bush, "Remarks by the President, 2002 Graduation Exercise of the United States Military Academy," West Point, N.Y., June 1, 2002. This text reappears as the epigraph of Section II, "Champion Aspirations for Human Dignity," of the National Security Strategy of the United States of America.

paign against terrorism is anything but novel. From the Declaration of Independence to the "axis of evil," American leadership has conceived of American interests in terms of universal virtue. On one level, even the Declaration of Independence was a permanent rebuke to realpolitik as well as to the kind of balance of power politics that defined the interest politics of Europe's competing nation-states. America's Declaration was intent on asserting the right of the thirteen colonies to do all those "Acts and Things which Independent States may of right do," including the "full Power to levy War" with "Reliance on the Protection of divine Providence." Even that familiar phrase in the Declaration's opening paragraph in which Jefferson alludes to a need to show "a decent Respect to the Opinions of Mankind" is introduced as part of a logic of declaring "the causes which impel [the colonies] to the Separation." That is to say, a respect for the opinions of mankind requires not that America do what mankind wishes it to do but only that it explain to mankind why it is doing precisely what it wishes to be doing.

America has been explaining its (often) unilateralist foreign policy decisions ever since, usually in terms of natural rights, American virtue, and Divine Providence. The "God bless America" with which every American politician ends every major address, above all those involving war and peace, acts as invocation and appeal: "fellow Americans, the United States acts in God's name!" and "Oh, God, please let it be so!" Like its great Protestant forebear Martin Luther, the United States declares itself to be constrained by its own conscience alone: "here we stand, and can do no other."

Exceptionalism, then, offers special rationalizations both for the isolationism that has tried to separate America from the world's tumult and for the interventionism that has pushed America out into its very heart. An idealist American foreign policy goes abroad in the name of the virtues of home and remakes the world in its own image not because it wants to dominate the world but because (it believes) it can only be safe in a world that is like America. Isolationism—an older, more conservative tradition—is no less wedded to the idea of American virtue, hoping, however, that a doctrine of independence secured by geography and arms (two oceans in the nineteenth century, an antiballistic missile shield in the twenty-first) will afford virtue the protection it requires. It may seem odd that a policy of reclusive separation from the world and a policy of aggressive intervention in the world are born of a single idea. Yet making the world safe for democracy has translated all too easily both into making America safe from the world and making America hegemonic in the world. In both cases, America prefers not to get "entangled" or to know the world too well.

PRESIDENT BUSH IS then on a two-century American roll when he inveighs today against the "axis of evil," calling for a worldwide war against "the evil ones" in the name of "the greatest nation, full of the most decent people, on the face of the earth," whose every action is to be seen not as that of a "conqueror" but that of a "liberator."[21] America's friends and allies may be appalled at the self-righteousness of this pulpit-pounding rhetoric. But for those who know America and its moralizing literature and have witnessed the impact of American morals on American politics, its tone is Puritan, exceptionalist, and moralizing in a familiar if exasperating American fashion. Bush may wear the six-guns of Gary Cooper's *High Noon* sheriff on his hips, but he carries a Methodist Bible under one arm and the Declaration of Independence under the

---

[21] "I was sensitive," said President Bush in his interview with Bob Woodward, "to this [accusation] that this was a religious war, and that somehow the United States would be the conqueror. And I wanted us to be viewed as the liberator" (*Bush at War*, p. 131).

other. No wonder he believes—as much of the nation believes with him—America will smite down the unrighteous and, however long it takes, emerge victorious in its war against the evil ones, if necessary, all by its lonesome self.

Such rhetoric is useful in rousing domestic audiences to support foreign wars for which they otherwise may have little stomach. Yet it is also more satisfying, and sometimes even more appropriate, than the skepticist language of mere national interest. After all, there was, minimally, a certain malevolence of hubris in the imperial aggressors of World War I, while the alliance formed by World War II's German-Italian-Japanese protagonists certainly permitted the United States to stipulate not merely an "axis" (as they were dubbed) but an "axis of evil." As for today, who among the thinking would wish to deny that there is evil in the machinations of nihilistic terrorists? Yet they are hardly the only evildoers on the planet, and terrorism is not some mutant seed nurtured in the Devil's own hothouse. It is a product of toxic ideologies and religious fanaticism, as well as of historical circumstances to which, given its extraordinary military, economic, and cultural power, the United States has to some degree contributed—whether inadvertently or through explicit imperialist ambition or, most probably, some confusing combination of both. There is also something unsettling in the parity of rhetoric that has al-Qaeda portraying America as an infidel nation doing the work of the Devil and America deploying analogous Old Testament language to condemn al-Qaeda as driven by evil ones (even if they *are* evil).

Terrorism may justify the president's rhetoric of moral blame but its logic demands also a responsive rhetoric of moral responsibility. Terrorism's agents may train in Taliban Afghanistan and find purpose in Allah's vengeance, but its impoverished admirers live in the slums of Karachi and the Gaza Strip and are reduced to taking solace from the "martyrdom" of their own children. If the first are to be vanquished, the second surely will have to be empowered. Disarming the Republican Guard in Iraq by itself does little to empower Saddam's subjects in Baghdad, let alone rescue the children of Palestine from despair.

The myth of innocence protects America, however, from the onerous burdens of historical responsibility for war or anarchy or injustice or conquest. A war on the Taliban shifts attention from urban slums in Gaza or angry refugees in Karachi. Yet to be so well protected by its ideals from the viewpoints of foreign cynics can blind it to solutions potentially more efficacious than those to which America has had recourse. Were Americans to listen not to some radical Baathist in Syria but to the motherly words of the nineteenth-century Englishwoman Frances Trollope (speaking to American social activist Fanny Wright way back in 1825), they would be chastised this way: "If the citizens of the United States were indeed the devoted patriots they call themselves, they would surely not thus encrust themselves in the hard, dry, stubborn persuasion, that they are the first and best of the human race, that nothing is to be learnt, but what they are able to teach, and that nothing is worth having, which they do not possess."[22]

Relying on a kind of secession from the foreign world of evildoers, or on the virtuous imposition of military vengeance upon them, diverts America from issues of causality and context. To insist the United States pursues only virtue where others pursue blunt interest robs America of realism in pursuing its aims. Attentive to its virtues, it too frequently neglects its interests. Intent on doing good, it sometimes fails to do very well either for others or itself.

This is not to suggest that America has been unsuccessful either as a fortress recluse (never so isolated as it pretended to be) or as a

[22] Quoted by Simon Schama, "The Unloved American: Two Centuries of Alienating Europe," *The New Yorker*, March 10, 2003.

world policeman (never so heavy-handed as its enemies made out). Walter Russell Mead surely has a point when he writes that compared "with the dismal record of the other great powers, American foreign policy . . . looks reasonably good."[23] But for a nation so powerful in a world without peers, "reasonably good" may not be enough. Mead himself sees dangers of "overreaching" that can have more disastrous consequences today than they had in the past, and he acknowledges (and this was before 9/11) that all is not well in America's attempt to cultivate an appropriate relationship to the new global order.[24] This is all the more true in an interdependent world where it is nearly impossible for the powerful not to overreach but where, thanks to exceptionalism, the American empire has been acquired in "a state of deep denial."[25]

The persistence of isolationist tendencies into the age of global interdependence is especially evident in America's pursuit of a missile shield—a touching remnant of the myth of innocence as applied to a technologically problematic strategic goal. President Ronald Reagan, as eloquent a spokesman for national innocence and national goodness late in his career as he was for General Electric in the early years, first dreamed of the technological cocoon that "star wars" supposedly proffered. As the two oceans once distanced America from the world's corruptions, technology was to

[23] Walter Russell Mead, *Special Providence: American Foreign Policy and How It Changed the World* (New York: Alfred A. Knopf, 2001), p. 11.

[24] Ibid., pp. 331, 332–34.

[25] Ignatieff, "The Burden." I find Ignatieff's use of the old term *empire* to portray America's new hegemony in a world without rivals unhelpful and even misleading, especially since he recognizes (as I argue here) that "despite its overwhelming military power" America "remains vulnerable," since its enemies are not states "susceptible to deterrence, influence and coercion, but a shadowy cell of fanatics who have proved that they cannot be deterred and coerced."

encapsulate the American people in a magic bubble through which those new foreign villains—the "evil empire" of communism for him, rogue states and scheming terrorists for his successors and for President Bush today—would be unable to penetrate. Never mind that America's diabolical enemies are more likely to use biological or chemical warfare, or transport dirty bombs on container ships or spray toxins from single-engine Cessna crop dusters or arm themselves with box cutters! Never mind that scientists are unanimous in arguing the system can't work. After all, even tests conducted under ideal circumstances that are unlikely to be replicated in time of war failed to achieve their goals.[26] Never mind, because the shield is as much a metaphor as a weapons system. Like those ubiquitous airport searches of old ladies separated from their shoes that signaled America's stiffening resistance to terror in the run-up to the Iraq war, the missile shield was more about show than action, valuable for what it told Americans about America (it will not be pushed around by terrorists!) rather than for what it did to terrorists and rogue states (interdict their mobility, intercept their missiles). Hence, in December 2002, regardless of the program's failure to meet the standard set by a handful of tests, President Bush ordered that the first stage of the antiballistic missile shield

[26] The tests that have been conducted have pitted an antiballistic missile against a single warhead ("a bullet trying to intercept a bullet") with at most a single decoy; but in reality, an aggressor will come with multiple missiles surrounded by multiple (inexpensive) decoys, making interception far more problematic than it already is, or it will use conventional delivery systems such as airplanes or boats. Such technical arguments are not, however, very useful in contesting what is, after all, more of a theology than a strategic defense doctrine. For the full controversy about the efficacy of missile defense, see the ongoing work of Professor Theodore A. Postol of MIT, who has waged a one-man campaign against what he argues are fundamental technical flaws in the antiballistic system and in MIT's studies of it. See, for example, William J. Broad, "MIT Studies Accusations of Lies and Cover-Up of Serious Flaw in Antimissile System," *New York Times*, January 2, 2003, p. A13.

be put in place—at a cost that would fund a Marshall Plan for the Muslim world.

The idea of an American technology rooted in American know-how that protects good from evil, innocence from corruption, Eden from the seething lands east of Eden, appeals deeply to America's exceptionalist core. Somewhere in that core Captain Amasa Delano still lives, oblivious to the heart of darkness to which—the rest of the world acknowledges—all humankind is subject. This America understands technology itself as an extension of its pragmatic nature and its marriage to progress: a nation of a can-do, fix-it-yourself people motivated by a potent combination of pragmatism and religious passion. Such a people can stand uncomprehending in the face of putative evil, blind to the lessons of mere national interest, certain of its own goodness, and thus intolerant of complexity. The vivid hues of red, white, and blue make it hard to see gray. And so America after 9/11—a lesson in realism if ever there was one—and America after Afghanistan and after Iraq—remains in many ways not only America the good and America the virtuous, but America the innocent.

3

The War of All Against All

... and the life of man [in the state of nature],
solitary, poor, nasty, brutish and short.
—*Thomas Hobbes, 1651*[1]

At some point we may be the only ones left. That's okay
with me. We are America.
—*President George W. Bush, 2002*

I f America can no longer insulate itself from the planet, the eagles say, then it must, in effect, rule the planet. If American sovereignty is compromised within its borders by a new interdependence that defies internal boundaries, America's borders must be extended to bring in and assimilate regions dangerous to the United States. Join us under the protective blanket or be destroyed. In portraying the new tactic of tracking commercial vessels that might be linked to terrorism, Frances Fragos-Townsend, chief of the U.S. Coast Guard intelligence service, observed, "if all you do is wait for ships to come to you, you're not doing your job, the idea is to push the borders out."[2] If the world has grown too

---

[1] *The Leviathan*, pt. 1, chap. 13.

[2] Quoted by John Mintz, "15 Freighters Believed to Be Linked to Al Qaeda," *Washington Post*, December 31, 2002, p. A1.

small for America to defend its universal rights in isolation, then America must become a universal presence: Q.E.D., Pax Americana.

This is the literal logic invoked by President Bush's push for hegemony at every level. Successful regime change in Iraq was not enough. The objective is not merely to rid the region of a brutal tyrant but to bring Iraq (and with it the Middle East) within America's borders through a kind of utopic Americanization under the guise of democratization. This looks to some like the kind of long-term "nation building" President Bush expressly condemned when running for the presidency prior to 9/11; it looks like empire building to others. The so-called reverse domino strategy sees in the wished-for "democratization" of Iraq the first of many democratic victories, country after country—helped along by M-1 tanks and F-18 fighters—falling into the American orbit.

If taken seriously (in a way realists generally will refuse to do), the appeal to democratization as the rationale for Pax Americana in Iraq and elsewhere can bring liberals aboard President Bush's battle cruiser. Middle-of-the-road liberal idealists such as Michael Walzer, Paul Berman, and Tom Friedman acquiesced to a war in Iraq with which they were clearly uncomfortable because it purported to bring to Iraqis the rights promised to all by the Declaration of Independence. If the logic of liberty that defined America's nationhood was common to all humanity, then perhaps war could again become liberty's tool as it had been in 1776. The question of whether either liberty or security in an age of terror can be won by war was of course at the heart of the debate about Iraq. Yet to see preventive war as a means to democracy is to misconceive both the consequences of aggressive war and the requirements for democracy's founding and development.

The challenge raised by Pax Americana is that in extending the logic of the Declaration of Independence by pushing out America's borders, it misunderstands the logic that lies behind the Declaration. For the Declaration of Independence that allowed a new and autonomous American experiment in democratic constitutionalism was also an expression of interdependence—of a social contract formed by the common will of its constituents.

In the political theory of the West that underlies European and American nation building, the social contract is a hypothetical compact between individuals who, in fact, renounce their "natural" independence as it applies to them one by one in a hypothetical "state of nature" in favor of a community of ends that allows them to create a nation. Free by nature (hence Jefferson's appeal in the Declaration to the natural rights to which men revert when the bonds of government are dissolved), people nonetheless find security for their freedom only under government. The social contract puts flesh on the bones of natural rights and muscle behind the idea of liberty. Free theoretically in the state of nature to do as we choose, we are exposed to the freedom of other men to do as they choose—which leave all in a condition of perpetual insecurity. More than anything else, today's global anarchy, in which terrorism and crime prosper and market capitalism escapes the bonds of democratic oversight, resembles this state of nature hypothesized in earlier social contract thinking.

Seventeenth- and eighteenth-century philosophers equated the state of nature with the human race's hypothetical history and used it to help explain and legitimize the founding of sovereign legal communities rooted in popular will. More than John Locke (with whom we are more familiar), Thomas Hobbes captured the fearfulness of the hypothetical state of nature that made escaping its painful struggles so pressing. In Hobbes's portrait in his great work *The Leviathan* (published following the English civil wars), the state of nature reflected an absence of all political institutions and social conventions. The state of nature was quite literally a condition of anarchy—like today's international realm—without government or law. As a consequence of Hobbes's unromantic portrait of the state of nature, his name is often invoked as a synonym for anarchy and his remedies are thought to involve brute force. Robert Kagan misreads him in exactly this fashion when he tries to persuade us that Europe lives in a "rule-based Kantian world" of would-be perpetual peace, while America makes its home in tougher neighborhoods under "the brutal laws of an anarchic Hobbesian world where power is the ultimate determinant of national security and success."[3] But Kagan gets Hobbes backward. As a consequence of its lawless anarchy, the state of nature is for Hobbes above all a state of fear—a condition of constant anxiety and perduring warfare where violence and conflict are more or less the whole of the human condition. The remedy is not power, which men have in the state of nature, but law and contract, which they lack.

Commentators suggest Hobbes used this hypothetical portrait of a "natural condition" at least in part to draw a picture of seventeenth-century England during the anarchy-inspiring civil wars (Stuarts and Puritans). He theorized and hypothesized conditions he had actually witnessed—anarchy, license, outlawry, fear, and uncertainty. In Hobbes's famously blunt portrait, this condition is one "of continual fear, and danger of violent death; and the life of man, solitary, poor, nasty, brutish, and short," but the point of politics is to get out as soon as a covenant can be contrived. The anarchy of the state of nature is literal: a condition of lawlessness where there are no governors, no agreements, no contracts and hence no property, no voluntary market exchanges other than those negotiated by force and fraud.

For Hobbes, these conditions dictated the necessity of politics and the indispensability of law. The "force and fraud" that ruled the

---

[3] Kagan, *Of Paradise and Power*, p. 37.

state of nature did not preserve men but destroyed them. In Hobbes they inspired a deep yearning for orderly government and turned him into a prophet of sovereignty based on consent. To be true to the language of Hobbes is to recognize that though Kagan's saber-rattling America may be from Mars, Mars is exactly what is wrong with the state of nature. Its reliance on force is part of the problem. Kagan's pacifist Europe, though it may be from Venus, is the key to Hobbes's solution, which involves an abjuring of private action and individual force in the name of a collective security yielded by the social contract.

As he captured the anarchy of the English civil wars with his vivid language depicting the "natural condition," Hobbes captures our own experience today of an international realm wracked with terrorist violence and Third World desperation, as well as with the First World fear and uncertainty they breed. Weak local government, poverty, and religious fanaticism constitute a recipe for uncertainty; international predators, whether they are financial speculators, drug syndicate criminals, or enraged terrorists, leave billions of people in the world in a state of perpetual fear, unable to govern their own destinies, as frightened of their own government and sometimes their own neighbors as they are of distant superpowers that intimidate them with their splendor and their hegemony. Terrorism has now displaced fear from the Third to the First World, giving those in Europe and America who have conquered anarchy within their own borders a taste of its grim rewards in the borderless world of interdependence that lies beyond.

Where anarchy was once the fate of women and men suffering from the lawlessness and disorder of the passage from medieval kingship to the early modern nation-state, anarchy is today the fate of those suffering from the lawlessness and disorder of the international realm. There, neither democracy nor, indeed, government of any kind are to be found—a state "of continual fear, and danger of violent death," not only for the luckless denizens of Third World ghettos but increasingly for trembling residents of privileged First World suburbs obsessed with what their television sets tell them terrorists may be planning for them.

Kagan and the eagles for whom he speaks would answer fear with fear, relying on force and fraud to dominate nature's anarchy. Yet fear is by its very definition terrorism's principal ally; its aim is precisely to draw its enemies into what Mark Juergensmeyer has called a "theater of terror" that can literally scare them to death.[4] It is the dark secrets of Hobbes's state of nature that the terrorists have discovered: in a world of fear and insecurity even the weakest can kill the strongest; fear of death can be more crippling than death itself; and to overcome insecurity, men may be tempted to forgo liberty—unless they can discover a formula in which they can abdicate nature's anarchy without surrendering their freedom. That formula is the social contract.

Only through the social contract can humankind secure civic liberty. Unlike natural liberty, which is universal in theoretical scope but narrowly limited in practical application, civic liberty sustains law and order. It secures the right to be safe through obedience to a common law that people participate in making: liberty, writes Rousseau, is obedience to a law we give to ourselves. People surrender the natural right they possess to liberty because such a right, possessed equally by others, puts all at risk. Instead they embrace

---

[4] Juergensmeyer, *Terror in the Mind of God*, p. 119. Juergensmeyer's book offers explanations for terrorism rooted in religious ideology and makes a useful contrast with views (like mine) emphasizing the dialectical complicity of McWorld and the West in terrorism's war against them. However, as Amy Chua argues in her *World on Fire: How Exporting Free Market Democracy Breeds Ethnic Hatred and Global Instability* (New York: Doubleday, 2003), it can also be shown (as I have tried to do in my *Jihad vs. McWorld*) "that the global spread of markets and democracy is a principal, aggravating cause of group hatred and ethnic violence throughout the non-Western world" (p. 9).

a social contract that replaces force and fraud with consensual obedience and democratic legitimacy. Why? Because we can guarantee both liberty and security through cooperation with others, even if it means surrendering the unrewarding independence of the natural condition.

The social contract, in effect, represents a refutation of the logic of personal independence. It replaces nature's personal declaration of independence ("I am free and can do as I will!") with a new declaration of interdependence ("my personal freedom is useless unless I cooperate with others to secure a common liberty and security for all"). Indeed, the social contract renouncing private independence is the condition for that later "collective" declaration of independence that proclaims the autonomous existence of a new sovereign social entity—the democratic nation-state.

Since the logic of social contract was thought by America's founders to have universal implications, extending to the whole planet, it has been the primary working basis for American foreign policy for the greater part of its history and the core premise of American policy in post–World War II Europe and Asia from the end of that conflict until September 11, 2001. The two great wars of the last century, as well as the bloody history of religious, economic, and political anarchy among nations that produced them, were in fact exactly what persuaded the United States that world peace could not be secured or sustained in the absence of viable international institutions defined by enforceable international laws.

As a consequence of this logic, in 1945 when (like today) it stood as an almost unrivaled hegemon and when some were counseling preventive war against its only potential rival (the Soviet Union), the United States instead became the chief architect of the United Nations and the principal supporter of multilateralism, European integration, and an approach to world peace that offered diplomacy and negotiation first, containment and deterrence second, and war only last—and even then (as in Korea), under the authority of the United Nations Charter.

In binding us to our own fear, terrorists effectively undo the social contract, bringing us full circle back to the Hobbesian "state of nature." For the last four hundred years, we have traveled a road from feudalism's breakup to the nation-state, from anarchy, insecurity, and fear to law and order—to lawful order, political safety, and the enjoyment of civil liberty. Yet the wars of the nineteenth and twentieth centuries and their accompanying genocides, the tribal and terrorist jihads of recent decades and the predatory conduct of free agents operating in anarchic international markets have over time reversed the arrows of liberty. Operating outside the law, making insecurity ubiquitous, and turning liberty into a synonym for risk, terror is the apotheosis of international anarchy, which in turn increases the attractiveness of brute repression.

Insecurity can drive nations to buy safety by sacrificing freedom. Repulsion at the ill-meant corrosive deeds of Osama bin Laden can create a tolerance for the well-meant corrosive deeds of John Ashcroft. An aggressive American attorney general willing to ride roughshod over the niceties of civil liberties for citizens as well as for noncitizens is less the product of a security-minded administration than of a badly frightened people. It was not Lincoln but his panicked Union constituents who made possible the suspension of habeus corpus during the Civil War; it was not Franklin Roosevelt but an alarmed American citizenry that facilitated the internment of loyal Japanese Americans in concentration camps during World War II. So too today, the enemy of civil liberties in the United States is not Ashcroft but fear. As it unhinges liberty from its moorings, terrorism succeeds in its mission of sowing dread.

In our fear of anarchy, we are actually returned to the anarchic state of nature that was fear's first true empire. There we feel obliged to abjure the law and rely on force and fraud alone; putting aside alliances and depending on ourselves; trading in the civil and lawful liberty acquired through democratic citizenship for that threadbare "natural liberty" that gives us the right to do what we can, to kill each other, in the name of self-preservation. We are drawn back into a war of all against all, and if not all, then all perceived "enemies." The list grows and grows: Iraq today, the "axis of evil" with North Korea and Iran included, tomorrow; Sudan, Syria, Indonesia, and Pakistan next week; Malaysia, Egypt, Saudi Arabia, Somalia, and the Philippines next year. In the state of nature there are finally no friends.

While there is much that is new in our current condition of global anarchy, there is also much that is old: the breakdown of civility and legal order as a consequence of civil strife and war (as during the English civil wars of the seventeenth century, for example), a sense of sovereignty's limits under conditions of terror and uncertainty (France, Russia, and Vietnam during their periods of revolution, for example); and the remarkable aptness of the metaphor of the "state of nature" in the international sector (during the last century's world wars, as well as today).

Now independent states constitute among themselves a new global "natural condition," defined by anarchy, force, and fraud. Independent states are as insecure with respect to one another as individuals once were in the state of nature. But what was clear for human relations within nation-states has been far harder to grasp for international relations. Nations are deluded by their nominal independence (this is the paradox of independence) into thinking that they have neither need of nor duty to one another.

Though international anarchy demands a compact among warring nations with even greater force than it called for a contract among warring individuals, today's two hundred nations continue to prefer the model of sovereignty. When they look to cooperation at all, they seek only a weak, less-than-binding form of balance of power politics that will not impair their individual sovereignties.

The idea of independence remains seductive. Interdependence feels like dependency, and dependency feels like the loss of liberty. Within the United States, many opposed the federalist vision of America for nearly a century, precipitating a violent civil struggle whose final cause was not the abolition of slavery but the integrity of federal union. The victor and the vanquished in that great struggle cannot always be told apart. In Thomas Dixon's work *The Clansman*, on which D. W. Griffith based his monumental and deeply racist 1914 film classic *Birth of a Nation*, a chapter on ejecting African Americans from the United States (what Griffith called "Lincoln's Solution") was entitled "Another Declaration of Independence."[5] The battle still rages today among Americans who prefer the confederal vision of an American nation as a congeries of semisovereign states whose powers are deemed to take priority over those of the central government (whose sovereignty exists only at the pleasure of the states) and those who actually accept that the United States is a sovereign nation whose whole is greater than and sovereign over its parts. That this states' rights perspective is still viable (and not without supporters on the U.S. Supreme Court), more than two centuries after the federal Constitution was ratified, suggests how hard it is to move from the idea of independent and autonomous sovereign states to something more encompassing— even within the American nation, let alone globally.

[5] The late Michael Rogin offers a brilliant and disturbing analysis of the relationship between Thomas Dixon, D. W. Griffith and Woodrow Wilson in his article " 'The Sword Became a Flaming Vision': D. W. Griffith's *The Birth of a Nation*," included in *Ronald Reagan, The Movie: And Other Episodes in Political Demonology* (Berkeley: University of California Press, 1987), pp. 194–95 in particular. His work is powerfully suggestive about the relationship between film, images, and American presidential leadership.

Some suggest that to realize supranational forms of sovereignty may first require the dissolution of nation-states; that it will be easier for individuals and subnational communities (already subordinate to nation-states and therefore accustomed to serving larger sovereign entities without losing their distinctive identities) to join together in a supranational community than for nation-states to do so. This suggests certain possible parallel strategies that proceed by incorporating cantons and provinces into regions larger than the nation-state: a "Europe" constituted not by France, Spain, and Germany, for example, but by their provincial regions like Catalonia, Provence, and Hesse. A North American Free Trade Association tying together California and the Baja peninsula more intimately than the United States and Mexico. An Africa woven together by tribes rather than by the often ineffective tribal conglomerates which occupying colonial powers created on the model of European nation-states.

Yet in places where nation-states have actually dissolved, such as ex-Yugoslavia or Afghanistan, the result has been instability and ethnic or tribal war rather than supranational integration of the fractious remnants. In the long term, nation-states remain the most powerful expressions of human community and the best guarantors of stability (if not always democracy). Moreover, because they are founded on the logic of interdependence (the logic of the social contract), they are equipped at least on paper with the means to achieve global forms of democratic governance. To the degree they fail to do so—in the absence of their engagement in building supranational forms of governance and international forms of legislation and cooperation—the natural anarchy that describes relations among nations is likely to become ever more destructive.

4

The "New" Doctrine of Preventive War

We cannot let our enemies strike first.
—*The National Security Strategy of the United States of America,*
September 2002

There is nothing more foolish than to think that war can be stopped
by war. You don't "prevent" anything by war except peace.
—*President Harry Truman*[1]

The Iraq war was the product of a strategic doctrine formally announced by Condoleezza Rice as the "National Security Strategy of the United States of America" on September 20, 2002. This doctrine appeared to be new, and yet was deeply rooted. It was probably formulated as a formal concept in the immediate aftermath of 9/11; it was adumbrated in a number of speeches by President Bush during the following year, most vividly at West Point in the spring of 2002, when the president warned, "we must take the battle to the enemy, disrupt his plans, and confront the worst threats before they emerge."[2] Its underlying logic goes back to a report on "Rebuilding America's Defense" prepared by the

---

[1] Cited from Truman's *Memoirs* in a letter from Mike Moore, editor of the *Bulletin of Atomic Scientists, New Republic,* November 4, 2002.

[2] Bush, "2002 Graduation Exercise of U.S. Military Academy."

Project for a New American Century, an informal group meeting in the late 1990s that included William Kristol, Robert Kagan, John Bolton, and others, many of whom are currently members of or advisers to the Bush administration.

The formal National Security Strategy paper is prefaced by a letter from President Bush putting its points in a nutshell. Conditions have changed fundamentally, the president concludes: "Enemies in the past needed great armies and great industrial capabilities to endanger America. Now, shadowy networks of individuals can bring great chaos and suffering to our shores for less than it costs to purchase a single tank. Terrorists are organized to penetrate open societies and to turn the power of modern technologies against us." This demands a fundamental change in strategy: America will now have to "act against such emerging threats before they are fully formed." This is a recipe for preventive war. Changed conditions— "America is now threatened less by conquering states than we are by failing ones. . . . We are menaced less by fleets and armies than by catastrophic technologies"—demand changed tactics: "The greater the threat, the greater is the risk of inaction—and the more compelling the case for taking anticipatory action to defend ourselves—even if uncertainty remains as to the time and place of the enemy's attack. To forestall or prevent such hostile acts by our adversaries, the United States will, if necessary act preemptively."

The document's logic assumes, quite correctly, American hegemony: "The United States possesses unprecedented—and unequaled—strength and influence in the world." More important, it assumes that hegemony is the American birthright and that peace requires it be maintained: "Our forces will be strong enough to dissuade potential adversaries from pursuing a military buildup in hopes of surpassing, or equaling, the power of the United States . . . we must build and maintain our defenses beyond challenge." But in the name of benign ends: American power will be deployed only to encourage "free and open societies" not to seek "unilateral advantage." In the exceptionalist spirit, this "rare union of our values and our interests" defines "a distinctly American internationalism."

According to the *Washington Post*, the full secret version of the doctrine "goes even further" and "breaks with 50 years of U.S. counter-proliferation efforts by authorizing preemptive strikes on states and terrorist groups that are close to acquiring weapons of mass destruction or the long range missiles capable of delivering them," the idea being to destroy parts before they are assembled.[3] The document's top secret appendix is reported to name Iran, Syria, North Korea, and Libya as well as Iraq among countries that will be the central focus of this new approach, and it pledges to "stop transfers of weapons components in or out of their borders."

Conceived as a response to new dangers, the preventive war doctrine introduces new risks. It intends to get beyond the shortcomings of the policies of deterrence and containment that defined the Cold War: "deterrence based only upon the threat of retaliation is less likely to work against leaders of rogue states more willing to take risks . . . traditional concepts of deterrence will not work against a terrorist enemy whose avowed tactics are wanton destruction and the targeting of innocents; whose so-called soldiers seek martyrdom in death and whose most potent protection is statelessness."[4]

Yet the new doctrine ends up reproducing some of containment's most perilous features. It assumes a certainty about events and their consequences that the history of events gainsays at every turning. George F. Kennan, America's foremost realist (now well

---

[3] Mike Allen and Barton Gellman, "Strike First, and Use Nuclear Weapons if Necessary," *Washington Post National Weekly Edition*, December 16–22, 2002.

[4] White House, The National Security Strategy of the United States of America, September 2002.

over ninety years old), said in a recent interview that anybody who has studied history understands "that you might start in a war with certain things on your mind," but the war rapidly becomes about things you "never thought of before."[5] By its logic of "anticipatory self-defense," the preventive war strategy relies on long-term prediction and a presumed concatenation of events far less certain than those appealed to by the immediate logic of self-defense. By shooting first and asking questions later, it opens the way to tragic miscalculation. By transgressing international law's traditional doctrine of self-defense, it sets a disastrous example for other nations claiming their own exceptionalist logic. And in abandoning the prudent logic of social contract and deference to law that was perhaps the finest achievement of American independence, it finally abjures the very idealist legacy in which it pretends to be grounded.

Cautious owls eying the long-term future of law and international order have protested. One remarked that the Bush administration, in its approach to the prisoners of the war on terrorism, "appears not to have understood, or cared to understand, that it had more legal arguments—and therefore, at least arguably, more legal options—than it brought to bear when it decided that Geneva, by and large, didn't apply or was too much trouble to apply. Here, as in its confrontation with the new International Criminal Court, which the administration is sworn to resist and has never recognized, it has shown zero interest in influencing the development of what is termed 'international humanitarian law,' as the law of war is euphemistically known nowadays."[6] Partisans of the empire of fear are persuaded that the capacity to shock and awe does far more to make men meek that all the law's vaunted majesty.

[5] Quoted in Albert Eisele, "Hill Profile: George F. Kennan," *The Hill*, September 25, 2002.

[6] Joseph Lelyfeld, "In Guantánamo," *New York Review of Books*, November 7, 2002.

Preventive war has some precedent in the history of America's international relations, but as officially promulgated doctrine it is a radical departure from the conventions of American strategic doctrine and actual warfare. The United States has certainly taken military action in the past without congressional approval and in a fashion that has been seen by some as hypocritical and by others as imperial. But it has always tried to root its right to deploy troops in the Constitution (the Tonkin Bay Resolution that legitimized the Vietnam War), in the United Nations Charter (Korea), or international law (Panama). It may have acted hypocritically but always paid the principles of law and self-defense the compliment of refusing to admit it was operating outside their compass.

Faced with Soviet Communism, a totalitarian threat more nefarious in the eyes of some Americans than German Nazism had been, preventive war was a constant temptation. President Truman's Secretary of the Navy Francis P. Matthews argued that the United States had to be ready "to pay any price, even the price of instituting a war to compel cooperation for peace," inaugurating a controversy about the advantages of a nuclear "first strike" that defined debates about preemption throughout the Cold War years.[7] Winston Churchill had contemplated opening a front against the Nazis from the Balkan underbelly of Europe in order to cut the Soviets off from war spoils in middle Europe. Some thought after the war concluded that America should finish off its erstwhile Russian "ally." Remarkably, much the same language of novel conditions and radically altered circumstances that have attended the promulgation of the preventive war doctrine after 9/11 was being used by Cold Warriors trying to persuade America that its more civilized views of warfare (after Hiroshima!) would have to be replaced by

[7] Letter from Moore, *New Republic.*

tougher thinking. In rationalizing the covert activities of the OSS in World War II, General James H. Doolittle was already pleading changed circumstances:

> It is now clear that we are facing an implacable enemy whose avowed objective is world domination by whatever means and at whatever cost. There are no rules in such a game. Hitherto acceptable rules of human conduct do not apply. If the United States is to survive, longstanding American concepts of "fair play" must be reconsidered. We must develop effective espionage and counterespionage services, and must learn to subvert, sabotage, and destroy our enemies by more clever, more sophisticated, and more effective methods that those used against us. It may become necessary that the American people become acquainted with, understand and support this fundamentally repugnant philosophy.[8]

President Bush might have borrowed this paragraph without changing a single word to craft the preface to his preventive war national security doctrine of September 20, 2002.

Once the Soviets acquired their own nuclear (and then thermonuclear) weapons, of course, prevention became more complicated (as it is today with North Korea). It became clear that the United States, if it waited to get hit, could never do more than "punish" the other side for its "victory" by destroying it in return. This was the mad logic of mutual assured destruction, or MAD, which tempted hawkish critics into thoughts of decisive preemption. Strategist Herman Kahn had calculated that even with the loss of forty or fifty million Americans, a first strike that put an end to the prospect of mutual annihilation could be deemed rational.

---

[8] Cited by Pat M. Holt, *Secret Intelligence and Public Policy: A Dilemma of Democracy* (Washington, D.C.: CQ Press, 1995), p. 239.

Throughout the Cold War, the calls for preemptive and preventive nuclear war against the Soviets never let up. They were parodied in scathing comedies of the era like *Dr. Strangelove, or How I Learned to Stop Worrying and Love the Bomb* and transmogrified into paranoiac fear in dramas like *Seven Days in May* and *On the Beach*. In the Cuban Missile Crisis of 1962 which was to test President Kennedy's nerve, the call for preemptive action was on the table for "rational" consideration. Kennedy actually faced the hard choice of launching a preventive strike against Cuba (after covertly installed Russian missiles were discovered there) in which Russians as well as Cubans would die and a nuclear exchange would be risked, or doing nothing and risking that the missiles—once operational—might be used in a first strike against the United States. Meanwhile, the Soviet Union was portrayed in the same moralizing language of evil ("totalitarian dictatorship" and the "empire of evil") that was recently deployed to justify preventive war against Iraq.[9]

President Kennedy ultimately chose compromise and diplomacy over preemption—despite the fact that the Soviet enemy possessed the means to annihilate the United States almost instantaneously—and managed to disarm Cuba of its Soviet missiles without war. Participants in those gut-wrenching days of decision agree that during the crisis the world came within a cat's whisker of Armageddon. It was saved not by prudent long-term strategic planning but only by the unexpected hands-on prudence of an aggressive American president and a belligerent Russian premier, helped along by

---

[9] It was common to argue that because the Soviet Union was "totalitarian" and not "authoritarian," it was invulnerable to being overthrown from the inside and would have to be vanquished from without. See, for example, Jeane Kirkpatrick, a one-time UN ambassador, "Dictatorships and Double Standards," *Commentary*, vol. 68, no. 5 (November 1979).

diplomatic legerdemain.[10] Following President Kennedy's prudent decision to opt for compromise, successive Democratic and Republican administrations (until recently) have chosen to stay with the more complicated and accommodating politics of multilateral diplomacy and containment and deterrence (risky enough in their own right).

Lex humana cannot then be written off as a policy for less perilous times in its refusal to accept "first strike" nuclear doctrines, or arguments for war not rooted in a "just war" cause or traditional self-defense (as specified in Article 51 of the United Nations Charter). It was the successful (if risky) response to far more dangerous times, when the United States faced enemies far more potent than al-Qaeda, let alone Iraq. The Soviets had weapons of mass destruction that were the real McCoy—serious nuclear and thermonuclear bombs—as well as the means to deploy them globally. They possessed an ideology of righteous historical wrath directed at capitalist democracies and at their leading agent, the United States. The attraction of an international legal system and a complex and often compromising system of alliances and treaties was that they were believed to afford protection against tyrannical enemies of law and order like the Soviets. They alone offered an alternative to the governance of fear implied in the "balance of terror" by which the peace was being kept.

---

[10] The matter was resolved peacefully only because both President Kennedy and Premier Khrushchev gave each other "second" chances (they both allowed an initially neglected peace offer "first letter" to be reinstated after a belligerent "second letter" threatening war had been sent); in doing so, they both had to resist the calls within their respective ranks for preventive strikes. See the full account in Ernest R. May and Philip D. Zelikow, eds., *The Kennedy Tapes: Inside the White House During the Cuban Missile Crisis* (Cambridge, Mass.: Harvard University Press, 1997).

The fears generated by 9/11 effectively destroyed the policy consensus of the Cold War period. Following its formal promulgation in Rice's national security statement, the logic of preventive war became the key to defending the threatened use of force against Iraq. In his October 8, 2002, speech to the nation on Iraq, the President declared that in light of the devastating attacks of 9/11, and "facing clear evidence of peril," America is unwilling to "wait for the final proof, the smoking gun, that could come in the form of a mushroom cloud." Having "every reason to assume the worst and . . . an urgent duty to prevent the worst from occurring," it simply cannot and will not resume "the old approach to inspections, and applying diplomatic and economic pressure."[11]

The new doctrine clearly liberated President Bush, allowing him to express as official policy the tough line he had been rehearsing for a year in cabinet meetings (in time it permitted him to forgo evidence altogether): "The time for denying, deceiving and delaying has come to an end," he now felt able to say. "Saddam Hussein must disarm himself or, for the sake of peace, we will lead a coalition to disarm him." Ever sensitive to the potent rhetoric of American exceptionalism, the president added that the United States was taking this position not simply to secure itself but to meet its "responsibility of defending human liberty against violence and aggression." And then on to the characteristic American apotheosis: "By our resolve we will give strength to others. By our courage we will give hope to others. And by our actions we will secure the peace and lead the world to a better day. May God bless America."

If President Bush was looking to anticipatory action against Taliban Afghanistan and Saddam's Iraq as a potent preventive response

---

[11] President George W. Bush, "Remarks by the President on Iraq at the Cincinnati Museum Center," October 8, 2003; cited in *New York Times*, October 9, 2002.

to terrorism, Paul Wolfowitz, perhaps the most hawkish and militant of the eagles in Rumsfeld's Pentagon, was looking for still more. Well before Rice drafted her document, he was seeking a policy of preemptive termination—quite literally "ending states who sponsor terrorism."[12] Rice's language in the new strategic document suggests that Wolfowitz's view prevailed. After all, Wolfowitz's boss, Secretary of Defense Donald Rumsfeld, was a champion of "thinking outside the box" of traditional defense doctrines. That might mean not just entertaining preemptive strikes, but whatever it takes to "end states" including assassination or even the poisoning of enemy food supplies—although if Bob Woodward is to be believed, this latter notion did not make it into the policy mix.[13] Assassination did, however, at least in administration rhetoric. Bush spokesman Ari Fleischer thus allowed as how if "the policy [in Iraq] is regime change," then "the cost of a one-way ticket is substantially less than [that of invasion]. The cost of one bullet, if the Iraqi people take it on themselves, is substantially less than that."[14]

Radical and new as these ideas may seem, the explicit logic of

[12] Woodward, *Bush at War*, pp. 60–61.

[13] Ibid., p. 100. In a column discussing the apparent willingness of President Bush to see Saddam Hussein killed, Nicholas D. Kristof argues that despite the ban on assassination signed by President Reagan (Executive Order 12333), the United States has engaged in covert assassination plans against selected adversaries more than a few times. The ban on it is not encoded in American law, and though Reagan's ban has been renewed since, it "can easily be nullified." Kristof argues that it at least "appears" that the U.S. government tried to kill Qaddafi of Libya in 1986, Mohammed Farah Aidid of Somalia in 1993, and Saddam Hussein in 1991. The real problem is "finding Saddam to kill him." See Kristof, "The Osirak Option," *New York Times*, November 15, 2002, p. A31. Ironically, although Baathist Iraq is gone, like Osama bin Laden, Saddam Hussein remains at large (as of June 2003).

[14] Ari Fleischer, press briefing in the James S. Brady Room, October 1, 2002.

preventive war was evident much earlier. National Security Presidential Directive 17 (also known as Homeland Security Presidential Directive 4), which was the first major policy collaboration of the National Security Council and the new Homeland Security Council chaired by Tom Ridge and which the President signed in May 2002, had announced that "traditional nonproliferation has failed, and now we're going into active interdiction." An administration official clarified the meaning of "active interdiction: it is "physical," he said; "it's disruption, it's destruction in any form, whether kinetic or cyber."[15]

Cofer Black, the CIA's counterterrorism deputy, spoke with equal audacity and far more relish on behalf of the spirit of the new doctrine and what it might entail. Although the attack on the Taliban could be construed in more traditional terms of self-defense, it also had an aspect of prevention (the Taliban had not attacked America, though their proxies had). Not long after 9/11, Black promised President Bush he would bring him Osama bin Laden's head; in case he was deemed to be kidding, he ordered boxes for the purpose when he embarked on his first mission to meet with Afghanistan's North Alliance as the war there got under way. "When we're through with [the Taliban and al-Qaeda], they will have flies walking across their eyeballs," he pledged, coining a phrase that captures the spirit not only of White House outrage at terrorist behavior but of preventive war itself, whose policies appear to be written in blood.

Although a year away from being formally proclaimed, the spirit of preemption was in the air immediately after 9/11. Black wanted everyone to know—this meant the Russians too, who might still regard Afghanistan as their turf—that America was on its way.

[15] Mike Allen and Barton Gellman, "Preemptive Strikes Part of U.S. Strategic Doctrine," *Washington Post,* December 11, 2002, p. A1.

"We're in a war, we're coming. Regardless of what you do, we're coming anyway." When the Russians responded with a warning about how America was likely to "get the hell kicked out of" it in Afghanistan, Black was unfazed: "We're going to kill them. We're going to put their heads on sticks. We're going to rock their world."[16] The hegemon was incensed. And as far as Afghanistan and Iraq were concerned, the hegemon was right. "This nation is peaceful, but fierce when stirred to anger," promised President Bush in his National Cathedral speech. It was no longer waiting for the bad guys to draw first. Mullah Omar was Osama bin Laden; the Taliban were Mullah Omar; the government of Afghanistan was the Taliban. America was no longer wedded to self-defense in the strict sense or civility in any sense at all. It no longer felt constrained to persuade others of the justice of its cause. Yes, it was respectful of "the values, judgment and interests of our friends and partners," but America was "prepared to act apart when [its] interests and unique responsibilities require."[17] As it would say again and again right through its war in Iraq, it needed no one's permission to identify and make preventive war on perceived enemies. The axis of evil and everyone vaguely associated with it had been put on notice. The only oddity is that the United States acted surprised when some of those put on notice reacted—like the North Koreans.

By the time the president gave his major policy address at the Citadel on December 11, 2001, the anger aroused by 9/11 in the president and in Rumsfeld, Wolfowitz, and Cofer Black had spawned the official term *active counterproliferation*. Counterproliferation meant no more reliance on treaties and promises; the nonproliferation treaty had failed and the Comprehensive Nuclear Test Ban Treaty had been found wanting. America itself

[16] Woodward, *Bush at War*, pp. 52 and 103.

[17] National Security Strategy.

had unilaterally withdrawn from the Antiballistic Missile Treaty. There would be no more pusillanimous efforts at bribing potential buyers of WMD; the Nunn-Lugar Program approved by Congress authorizing the buying up of loose nukes in the ex-Soviet territories had been effectively defunded.[18] Rather, what counterproliferation meant was preemptive strikes against facilities being used for the development of weapons of mass destruction. A heavy club in place of the carrot, wielded not as a deterrent but as a preemptive punisher of potentially bad children. Counterproliferation was a euphemism for preventive war, active interdiction of potential delinquency by fed-up parents no longer willing to wait to find out what the kids were going to do next.

Preventive war, driven by fear and uncertainty, replaced the indicative logic of self-defense ("we've been attacked!") with a new subjunctive logic ("someone may be preparing to attack us"). Self-defense says: "We are already at war thanks to our enemies: our declaration of war is but a confirmation of an observable condition." Preventive war says: "It is a dangerous world where many potential adversaries may be considering aggression against us or our friends, or may be acquiring the weapons that would allow them to do so should they wish to: so we will declare war on that someone and interdict the possible unfolding of this perilous chain of could-be's and may-be's."

It is immediately clear that the effects of threats of preventive war are not always what is intended. Blustery war rhetoric is of course a specialty of the isolated regime of Kim Jong Il, but rhetorical war is usually a two-way street. In identifying North Korea as a charter member of the axis of evil, President Bush effectively identified it as a potential target of the new preventive war strategy. In

---

[18] Only after protests from Democrats and Republicans alike was the program refunded in the months before the war in Iraq.

calling Kim Jong Il a "pygmy" whom he "loathed," the president identified him as an adversary as repugnant as Saddam Hussein, someone "next" on the "one at a time" serial preventive war target list. How is a nation targeted as a candidate for "assisted suicide" (the term some use to describe the administration's "tailored containment" plan that awaits the collapse of a bankrupt North Korea) likely to react to such bluster? Is it surprising that, as Bill Keller has written, they "have taken our bellicose talk fairly seriously"? Especially when "we abruptly cut off discussion, adopt military 'pre-emption' as our doctrine for dealing with nuclear wannabes, and cite North Korea as a justification for building a missile defense system in Alaska."[19]

It should not be surprising that North Korea has been panicked by this logic and its inflammatory rhetoric into a state of genuine fearfulness. Whatever America may be saying now, North Korea surely reckons it is next on the axis of evil hit list—but at a time and place America will select when its war on Iraq is over.[20] Why else the axis of evil? Why else a contingency plan to go nuclear against it in the name of eliminating its nuclear capabilities? Why else dozens of B-1 and B-52 bombers ordered to Guam in early 2003?

---

[19] Bill Keller, "At the Other End of the Axis: Some F.A.Q.'s," *New York Times*, January 11, 2003, p. A15. Of course, as Keller acknowledges, it was the Koreans who first broke the 1994 "Agreed Framework" in which North Korea agreed to end its nuclear program in return for American assistance, two light water reactors (much harder to process weapons-grade plutonium from), and assured nonaggression from the United States. This agreement, brokered by President Carter working as an emissary for President Clinton, ended a crisis very much like the current one, in which Clinton actually entertained the idea of a strike against the nuclear facility prior to striking the deal. North Korea broke its bargain in 2002, although it hasn't yet received the pledged light water reactors.

[20] This is the clear implication of the president's words in his National Cathedral address, September 14, 2001, when he declared that while "this conflict was begun on the timing and terms of others, it will end in a way, and at an hour, of our choosing."

Why else the refusal to negotiate bilaterally with North Korea when its aim appears to be pushing the United States to the bargaining table rather than into war?

Similarly, CIA chief George Tenet testified to the Senate Committee on Intelligence (February 11, 2003) that Iran remained a serious concern because of its support for terrorism—the very charges that led America to invade Iraq. In the view of one observer, this militarization of policy leaves the U.S. government "increasingly dependent on its military to carry out its foreign affairs,"[21] which in turn convinces Thomas Powers that "the implication seems clear: Iraq first, Iran next."[22] According to Paul Krugman of the *New York Times*, a British official with ties to the Bush team reported that "Everyone wants to go to Baghdad. Real men want to go to Tehran."

Israel under Prime Minister Ariel Sharon shares the view. Ranan Lurie of the Center for Strategic and International Studies in Washington explains Sharon's perspective this way: "It is inconceivable that [the United States] will attack Iraq, succeed, destroy its unconventional laboratories and arsenal, come home for a ticker-tape parade on Wilshire Boulevard and go to the beaches while Iran is still there. Imagine a brain surgeon penetrating the skull of a patient who has two malignant tumors and yet extracting only one of them. Logic says that, as long as you are in that skull, the same incision should serve for the removal of the second tumor."[23] As if to give impetus to this logic, Iran announced in

[21] Dana Priest, *The Mission: Waging War and Keeping Peace with America's Military* (New York: W. W. Norton, 2003), p. 14.

[22] Thomas Powers, "War and Its Consequences," *New York Review of Books*, March 27, 2003.

[23] Cited in Mansour Farhang, "A Triangle of Realpolitik: Iran, Iraq and the United States," *The Nation*, March 17, 2003. Farhang notes that Sharon has urged President Bush to go after Iran "the day after [he] finishes off Saddam Hussein."

March 2003 that (like North Korea) it had embarked on an aggressive nuclear energy program of its own that might be used to produce weapons-grade plutonium, while President Bashar al-Assad insisted America's war in Iraq was intended to "redraw the map of the region" and that Syria was a potential target. Meanwhile, some conservatives who had pushed for war in Iraq were "already moving on to the next step, and perhaps farther than the President is ready to go," calling Iraq the opening of a "Fourth World War" (the Cold War having been, in their view, the third).[24]

Preventive war doctrine has domestic as well as foreign policy consequences. As it trumps traditional self-defense arguments and permits more aggressive moves abroad, it trumps civil liberties arguments and permits more aggressive moves at home. The same logic of special circumstances, novel adversaries, and altered technology used to legitimize preventive war is used to rationalize preventive detention. As Joseph Lelyveld articulates the argument (on the way to criticizing it),

> Jihadists are different from other warriors, in that their struggles won't obviously be ended by an armistice or surrender proclaimed from on high. The overriding objective of any detention regime in these circumstances has to be the gathering of intelligence about the network and its targets that may serve to prevent future attacks. Prevention is more important than prosecuting individuals for past actions. If you are looking to the future, it's hard to say who among the detainees is important—that is, danger-

---

[24] David E. Sanger citing former CIA director R. James Woolsey, "Viewing the War as a Lesson to the World," *New York Times*, April 6, 2003, p. B1. Sanger reports that in the first week of April 2003, when an aide warned President Bush that "his unpredictable Defense Secretary has just raised the specter of a broader confrontation [with Syria and Iran]," President Bush "said one word—'Good'—and went back to work."

ous—and who's not. If future actions are the primary concern, it would be reckless to release persons who have already shown themselves to be adherents of movements that directly or indirectly supported the suicide attackers of September 11.[25]

To be sure," as even Paul Wolfowitz admits, many of the detainees may "turn out to be completely harmless." But "if we put them in the Waldorf Astoria, I don't think we could get them to talk."[26] This is, of course, the slippery slope logic that has led Alan Dershowitz to consider the legitimacy of "legal" torture in the age of terrorism.[27]

The subjunctive logic of prevention, so crucial to the recent changes in both foreign and domestic policy that have unsettled European friends of the United States, patently lay behind America's preoccupation with nations like Iraq and North Korea after 9/11. But such thinking animated other presidents well before President Bush pointed to an axis of evil and promulgated a doctrine of preventive war. The Clinton administration, for example, had contemplated a preemptive strike against the North Korean nuclear processing plant at Yongbyon during its first term and actually delivered a preventive blow against what it mistakenly believed was a Sudanese chemical weapons plant during its second (in 1998). The logic of prevention was codified in Clinton's Presiden-

---

[25] Lelyveld, "In Guantánamo."

[26] Lelyveld quoting Paul Wolfowitz. Lelyveld's "Waldorf-Astoria" quote is from an unnamed officer.

[27] Alan M. Dershowitz, *Why Terrorism Works: Understanding the Threat, Responding to the Challenge* (New Haven: Yale University Press, 2002). See chap. 4, "Should the Ticking Bomb Terrorist Be Tortured?" Dershowitz would legalize torture only when it seemed likely that it would be deployed illegally anyway, asking for "a formal requirement of a judicial warrant as a prerequisite to nonlethal torture" (p. 158). Better under legislative and judicial oversight than in the dark of foreign prisons like the one at Guantánamo Bay.

tial Decision Directive 62 aimed at "Protection Against Unconventional Threats to the Homeland and America Overseas." A former Clinton administration official summarizes the directive's classified language in this syntactically challenged way: "If you think terrorists will get access to Weapons of Mass Destruction, there is an extremely low threshold that the United States should act militarily."[28]

In fact, there is nothing partisan in this new doctrine. In its 2000 Party platform, the Democratic Party suggested that an evolving international environment called for a new doctrine of "forward engagement" that would "mean addressing problems early in their development before they become crises, addressing them as close to the source of the problem as possible, and having the forces and the resources to deal with these threats as soon after their emergence as possible."[29] Forward engagement is not preventive war, but it is not exactly traditional self-defense either.

President Clinton had in fact himself voiced many of the same fears with respect to Iraq and the need for interdiction that President Bush would articulate four years later. In a statement frequently cited by the Bush administration, Clinton had warned that the "predators of the 21st century will be all the more lethal if we allow them to build arsenals of nuclear, chemical and biological weapons and the missiles to deliver them . . . there is no more clear example of this threat than Saddam Hussein's Iraq." Sounding more like Bush than either Bush or Clinton would probably wish, Clinton ended his peroration by warning that if the United States failed to act, Saddam would "conclude that the international com-

---

[28] Allen and Gellmann, "Preemptive Strike."

[29] Congressman Norman Dicks of Washington, speech at the second session of the 43rd Democratic Convention, August 15, 2000, in Los Angeles, California; cited in sidebar, *New Republic*, September 23, 2002.

munity has lost its will. He will then conclude he can go right on and do more to rebuild an arsenal of devastating destruction. And some day, some way, I guarantee you, he'll use the arsenal."[30]

Even before President Clinton, there is strong evidence that Dick Cheney, in his guise as President George H. W. Bush's secretary of defense back in the late 1980s, was already urging a preemption option. In a document known as the Defense Planning Guidance, Cheney argued "that the United States should be prepared to use force if necessary to prevent the spread of nuclear weapons . . . (and should) maintain United States military primacy and discourage the emergence of a rival superpower."[31] These ideas were controversial at the time, and not embraced by Bush *père*. Their time had to await Bush *fils* and the shock of 9/11.

Given the President's disposition to moralizing language, it is interesting that the Bush doctrine does not invoke the concept of just war; nor did the Clinton administration or its Cold War predecessors. Just war debates turn on religious and moral arguments with a universal compass and such arguments are quite distinctive from preventive war doctrine.[32] Arguments for humanitarian intervention, however, have sometimes been confounded with arguments for prevention. But humanitarian interventionism is sui generis. Unlike the American argument for preventive war, it is not based on exceptionalist claims and it works best when framed by

[30] Jonathan Chait, "False Alarm: Why Liberals Should Support the War," *New Republic*, October 21, 2002.

[31] Michael R. Gordon, "Serving Notice of a New U.S., Poised to Hit First and Alone," *New York Times*, January 27, 2003, p. A1.

[32] For the best philosophical account of just war debates, see Michael Walzer's *Just and Unjust Wars: A Moral Argument with Historical Illustrations* (New York: Basic Books, 1977). For a just war discussion of terror, see Jean Bethke Elshtain, *Just War Against Terror: The Burden of American Power in a Violent World* (New York: Basic Books, 2003).

multilateralism and international law (which recognizes the rights of peoples subjected to persecution and genocide—hence the Genocide Convention). The Rwandan tribal war between Hutus and Tutsis (aggravated by aggressive government media) and the Balkan "ethnic cleansing" campaigns are perhaps the two most familiar recent instances where liberal internationalists (David Rieff and Michael Ignatieff, for example) believed there were good reasons for American (and/or European and United Nations) intervention, despite the absence of any direct threat to the United States or its interests.

Yet while some proponents of humanitarian intervention ended up supporting the invasion of Iraq on grounds of humanitarianism (Saddam Hussein was, after all, a monstrous oppressor), the argument for humanitarian intervention and the argument for American preventive war are distinct. For humanitarian interventionism embodies a doctrine that can be made universal: it calls on every state and on the international system to intervene and does so not to protect the intervening state but to protect others who are unable to protect themselves.

The humanitarian argument was used as a fallback position by the Bush administration in Iraq (Saddam was a brutal tyrant and had used chemical weapons during his war against Iran; overturning his regime was an act of charity to the Iraqis), but it is clear that preventing terrorism through disarmament, interdicting the threat of weapons of mass destruction, and regime change were the primary arguments and that in their absence neither the American public nor the administration itself would have supported a "merely" humanitarian war. Going to war with Iraq was a clear consequence of 9/11 and the unique circumstances and special obligations created on that fateful day—which putatively endowed the United States with a special right to preventive war that other nations (say India facing Pakistan over Kashmir) could not claim.

Just war theorists might of course claim that America's high ideals generate a special obligation for it to participate in humanitarian wars against tyrants who may otherwise be of no threat to the United States, but they would argue that other nations have the same obligations. Preventive war theorists, on the other hand, claim that America's special destiny permits it to pursue policies aimed at disarming potential adversaries and democratizing potential tyrants because its own existence is special and worthy of special measures—a rationale not permitted to other nations. In general, just war arguments are rooted in universal principles that make exceptionalist arguments more difficult to employ: in theory, every nation, regardless of culture or special character, has an obligation, say, to end genocide in Rwanda or deter ethnic cleansing in Kosovo—nothing exceptionalist here. But when the French adduce from their (self-described) unique relationship with civility an obligation to civilize other nations (*la mission civilatrice*) or when Rudyard Kipling infers a noblesse oblige which allowed Britain to rationalize its colonies or when Teddy Roosevelt alludes to America's racial superiority as a justification for its wars of colonial liberation against Spain, something other than just war theory is at stake. Moral right here is being adduced from special character, not from universal principle. Thus, when the United States invoked special virtue or manifest destiny on the way to building an empire, exceptionalism rather than just war theory was at stake. Rudyard Kipling, if not President Bush, at least understood that exceptionalism had few rewards other than its own virtue. To "take up the White Man's burden," Kipling wrote could only be to

> *. . . reap his old reward—*
> *The blame of those ye better,*
> *The hate of those ye guard.*

From the American perspective, exceptionalism means other nations have no particular right to deploy preventive strategies of their own. But from the perspective of other countries, America's embrace of the preventive doctrine established a significant precedent, especially since America sees itself as a standard-bearer and standard-setter for the world community. Based on the American model, but disregarding America's claim that its right to preemption is rooted in unique circumstances, Pakistan can argue for preventive war against India, anticipating an Indian strike in Kashmir; North Korea can justify a strike against South Korea, anticipating an American action (based on American rhetoric) against North Korea; or, for that matter, Iraq could have rationalized a preventive strike against the United States or its allies, anticipating what was, after all, a well-advertised American intention to launch a war against Baghdad. Comical perhaps, but in the interest-constrained world of international relations, why should Saddam Hussein not borrow America's preemptive doctrine? He could claim with conviction that the United States was bent on war against his government, that it had weapons of mass destruction and was intent on acquiring more, and was led by a government manifestly hostile to Iraq. Either change your regime, America, and renounce your weapons of mass destruction, or face a preventive Iraqi strike!

Less comically, as I have already shown, North Korea seems to be engaging in something very much like preventive war strategy when it perceives in various American positions deep hostility to its very existence as a regime. Coupled with the American unwillingness to negotiate, this adds up to an aggressiveness sufficient to have caused the North Koreans to threaten a kind of preventive "catastrophe" of their own: the reopening of their plutonium processing plants and the renewed effort to produce nuclear weapons.

The defect of exceptionalism, then, is that it assumes America's allies and even its enemies will share the special-case reasoning that persuades America it possesses unique extralegal prerogatives based on its exceptional righteousness. Even if there are reasons to think the United States has acted more virtuously in its foreign affairs than most nations, American virtue can hardly be accepted by others as a universal standard. Imagine an international law that read, "Nations may only resort to war in cases of self-defense, except the United States, which because it is special can resort to war whenever it wants." It may be difficult for Americans to read their own doctrine in this skeptical manner, but it will be far less difficult for America's adversaries and even some of its friends to do so. Indeed, America's inability to see its own motives through this lens is why it is often viewed as arrogant even by its friends and allies.

But the more serious problem with the argument pointing to America's democratic virtue is not that it provides hypocritical cover for base national interests (although as William James insists, it certainly may) but that even where virtue can be demonstrated the doctrine fails the basic test of international legality. Exceptionalism can never meet the Kantian principle (after the eighteenth-century philosopher Immanuel Kant) which requires that the morality or legality of a precept be measured by its susceptibility to being universalized. If preventive war is moral for America, everybody else has America's right to preventive self-defense (just as everybody else has America's right to self-government and democracy). Or, if America denies others that right, its own resort to prevention cannot be morally justified. The whole point of exceptionalist reasoning is to exempt the United States from universal precepts with respect to war. It wants to persuade others that because it is uniquely moral, its policies must be ethical. But moral precepts are supposed to define moral agents, not the other way around.

Bush's preventive war doctrine postulates America's right to take steps against perceived enemies before they actually strike at America. In order for it to gain acceptance outside the United States, we have seen, it must be generalized to meet the Golden

Rule standard of "do onto others." Germany, Russia, Pakistan, and yes, even Iraq and North Korea, must have the same right to pre-empt what they perceive as potential or imminent aggression against them by their enemies. Of course, as the United States knows, that way lies only anarchy: each nation deciding on war whenever and wherever it sees fit. The doctrine not only fails the test of legality, it fails the test of realism. For no nation, not even one as powerful as America, can root its foreign policy in special reasoning forbidden to others. No nation can realistically succeed in an interdependent world unless it somehow secures its permanent dominion over the entire planet, something no nation in an interdependent world can possibly do.

5

The "Old" Doctrine of Deterrence

> The President has no intention of allowing any
> foreign power to catch up with the huge lead
> the United States has opened since the fall of
> the Soviet Union more than a decade ago. . . .
> Our forces will be strong enough to dissuade
> potential adversaries from pursuing a military
> build-up in hopes of surpassing, or equaling,
> the power of the United States.
>
> —*The National Security Strategy of the
> United States of America, September 2002*

> We cannot consider that the armed invasion and occupation of
> another country are peaceful means or proper means to achieve jus-
> tice and conformity with international law.
>
> —*President Dwight Eisenhower, 1957*[1]

The national security doctrine offers an explicit contrast to the age of deterrence, observing that: "In the Cold War, especially following the Cuban missile crisis, we faced a generally status quo, risk-averse adversary. Deterrence was an effective defense. But

---

[1] President Eisenhower, who had opposed Europe's and Israel's 1956 invasion of Egypt, was here criticizing Israel's continued (partial) occupation of Egypt after France and Britain, under American pressure, had withdrawn.

deterrence based only upon the threat of retaliation is less likely to work against leaders of rogue states more willing to take risks, gambling with the lives of their people, and the wealth of their nations." Although there were a number of American strategic planners in the 1940s and 1950s who regarded first the Nazis and then the Soviets as anything but "status quo, risk-averse" adversaries, President Bush's account of radically altered circumstances nonetheless retains a certain conviction. As the president said in a January 2003 press conference, "after September 11, the doctrine of containment just doesn't hold any water."[2] Couple this with the reality that once acquired, technologies of mass destruction can impose instant costs, and it is evident why President Bush might suggest that if America awaits hard evidence to prove the intentions of a terrorist adversary, it could come in the shape of a mushroom cloud—a signal for which he was unwilling to wait.

President Bush's National Security Strategy paper notes that traditional self-defense concepts did recognize "imminent threat" as a possible basis for preemption; but imminent threat was traditionally understood as "a visible mobilization of armies, navies, and air forces preparing to attack." Under the novel conditions of a world beset by terrorists, however, the United States "must adapt the concept of imminent threat to the capabilities and objectives of today's adversaries. Rogue states and terrorists do not seek to attack us using conventional means. They know such attacks would fail. Instead, they rely on acts of terror and, potentially, the use of weapons of mass destruction—weapons that can be easily concealed, delivered covertly, and used without warning." Under such circumstances it is clear that "the United States cannot remain idle while dangers gather." To do so, in the phrase of prominent

[2] President George W. Bush, press conference with Prime Minister Blair, January 31, 2003.

Department of Defense eagle Paul Wolfowitz, would be a "reckless gamble."[3]

Yet for all the special pleading, when it comes to reckless gambles how different is the logic of preventive war from the logic of deterrence? As an instrument of direct action against terrorists it is clearly very different. Terrorists and their organizations are and must be regarded as fair game. To use Hobbes's imagery, they have put themselves back in the "state of nature," where any individual or group or nation has a right to strike them down before they can take a hostile action. Hence, the Bush administration's war on terrorism that proceeds against suspected terrorists through assassination, interdiction, arrest, detention, and expropriation of their financial and communication assets would appear to be fully justified, at least once an initial terrorist aggression has been perpetrated. This aggression puts the perpetrators quite literally at war with America (and other nations they strike) and justifies, even in the name of traditional self-defense, the use of every weapon against them without awaiting another attack or definitive proof that loosely linked individual terrorists or terrorist cells are individually or personally responsible for acts under the ideology of annihilation to which they subscribe. Such global terrorist organizations are bound to violence by radical commitments and fundamentalist ideology; they are wholesale criminals who have put themselves altogether outside of the sovereign state system; they are self-declared warriors in terrorism's assault on America.

The war on terrorism is not then really a preventive war at all. As President Bush rightly noted in responding to a supposed leak after 9/11 about how he had already surreptitiously "begun" a war, "they

---

[3] "What Does Disarmament Look Like?," address to the Council on Foreign Relations, New York, January 23, 2003.

don't get it, the war already began. It began on September 11."[4] Preventive war against terrorists is reactive, since it is only the terrorists' overt act (or acts) that identify adversaries as terrorists in the first place. America's war on terrorism is in fact a responsive conventional war (if by unconventional means) against an aggressor who has already shown Americans the "smoking gun."

The problem for the preventive war doctrine comes when the appropriate logic of a war against terrorists whose acts are known even when their origins are not is applied to states whose addresses are known though their connections with terrorism are not. Here the subjunctive logic of preventive war comes into play, raising questions about its slippery slope reasoning, the reasoning that constantly moves it from certainty to uncertainty, from claims that "our enemy has committed aggression" to "our enemy might/could/may commit aggression." Preventive war as a doctrine is designed to apply to known terrorist perpetrators who have committed aggressive and destructive acts but whose location and origins remain uncertain; it has been applied however, to states whose location is known and identity obvious even though their connections to actual aggression is far less certain. Terms like *states that harbor* or *states that sponsor* terrorism are used in place of explicit causal explanations that would show such states to be actual or even imminent aggressors. To make sovereign states—themselves self-evidently inappropriate candidates for preventive war—appear more appropriate targets, fuzzy terms like *rogue state* are introduced that putatively link states that can be militarily defeated to terrorists who are far more elusive.

Immediately following September 11, 2001, President Bush declared war on terrorism. On March 17, 2003, in announcing the

---

[4] Quoted by Woodward, *Bush at War*, p. 280.

American invasion of Iraq, unsupported by the United Nations, he declared that to wait a moment longer would be "suicide," adding that "the security of the world requires disarming Saddam Hussein now." How he got from the first widely supported goal of suppressing terrorism to the second widely opposed goal of removing Saddam from power is at least in part a story of fear—fear instilled by awful terrorist deeds but also fear marketed and amplified by the administration's response to terror. On its slippery slope, "rogue states" became fixed targets that could be identified, located, and attacked, but targets that were stripped of their internationally recognized sovereign rights, which otherwise should have protected them from attack. These rights were forfeited because of the "rogue" label, suggesting that the target states were not fully legitimate sovereign entities with a right to govern their own territory and people. In the period immediately before the Iraq war began, the Bush administration took to referring to Iraq as not only a "rogue state," but also a "terrorist state." In the same period, Secretary of Defense Rumsfeld referred to North Korea as a "terrorist regime."[5]

This greased logic—which allows attention to slip from nonstate terrorist agents to state "sponsors" of terrorism—opens up a world of uncertainty with respect to causality, predictability, and certainty. While the new national security doctrine argues persuasively that it is precisely the novel "statelessness" of terrorist aggressors that makes them immune to deterrence, terrorist sponsors (where they can be clearly shown to be such) are obviously not "stateless" but the very opposite. States are vulnerable: they have fixed assets,

---

[5] President Bush used the phrase "terrorist state" for Iraq in his joint appearance with Secretary of State Powell the day after Powell's February 2003 Security Council speech. Rumsfeld's comment was reported in the *New York Times* on February 7, 2003 (James Dao, "Nuclear Standoff: Bush Administration Defends Its Approach to North Korea," p. A13).

high-value targets, conventional armaments, and enduring interests including self-preservation. Possessing these traditional attributes, they are perfectly suitable candidates for the very deterrence and containment doctrines being eschewed by the American government.[6] To apply a national security doctrine developed for "stateless martyrs," who have actually started a war through terrorist acts, to a territorial state otherwise innocent of an explicit aggressive act is more than just incoherent: it is defective, inefficacious, even perverse. The widespread opposition to the war in Iraq prior to its unfolding as a fait accompli arose out of precisely these concerns.

The slippage here from nonstate terrorists to states is hardly accidental. Terrorists are difficult even to find, let alone to defeat, especially by conventional weapons of the kind that define a mod-

[6] Former CIA analyst Kenneth Pollack has suggested that deterrence, which was such a "reasonable alternative" in dealing with "the Soviet Union for 45 years," cannot work in Iraq because Saddam Hussein is "unintentionally suicidal." Indeed, because "his calculations are based on ideas that do not necessarily correspond to reality and are often impervious to outside influences" and given his "history of catastrophic miscalculations," the only question the United States faces is "war now or war later—a war without nuclear weapons or a war with them" ("Why Iraq Can't be Deterred," *New York Times Magazine*, September 26, 2002). For details, see his *The Threatening Storm: The Case for Invading Iraq* (New York: Random House, 2002).

On the contrary, one can suggest that Saddam Hussein's regime survived for thirty-one years not as a result of "good luck" (Pollack's candidate for explanation) but because Saddam has read and responded to external carrots and sticks very well. The Iraq aggression against Kuwait—his major "miscalculation"—originated as much from a lack of clear American intentions (the American ambassador to Iraq in 1991 waffled when she should have warned Iraq of dire consequences) as from his own irrationality, a thesis fortified by his responsiveness to American nuclear threats if he deployed biological and chemical weapons in that war. More important, Pollack actually makes the case for the difference between states with interests and terrorists by trying to exempt Hussein from its otherwise convincing logic. Since in the end the threat of preventive war failed to deter Saddam, it failed to do what the Bush administration hoped it would do.

ern superpower like the United States. In Bob Woodward's account, Secretary of Defense Rumsfeld was frustrated in the early days of the campaign in Afghanistan by the fact that "the target list cannot impose much damage on the people we want to impose it on." He was joined in his complaint by General Richard B. Myers, who observed, "we've got a military that does great against fixed targets. We don't do so well against mobile targets."[7] Their concern was the Taliban regime, but their comments point to the difficulty of confronting terrorism with conventional weapons when the real enemies have "networks and fanaticism" rather than "high-value targets."[8]

On the other hand, as what on paper was the best armed state among the Arab nations, the Iraqis (before the war) had 36,000 elite troops and a hundred thousand or more others, 200 battle tanks, 316 airplanes, up to 90 choppers, and up to 3,000 antiaircraft guns. Impressive as it was, such conventional weaponry matched up with and thus could be destroyed by America's superior firepower with relative ease—as, in fact, it soon was. In thinking about strategy, Vice-President Cheney argued, apparently without irony, that "to the extent we define our task broadly, including those who support terrorism, then we get at states. And it's easier to find them than it is to find bin Laden."[9] Like the drunk looking on the wrong side of the street for the keys he dropped on the other side because "the light is better over here," the United States prefers the states it can locate and vanquish to the terrorists it cannot even find. American military superiority depends on weapons commensurability: when its adversaries have the same kind of weapons, but fewer of them and less technologically evolved and expertly deployed than America's, its victory is assured.

---

[7] Woodward, *Bush at War*, p. 174.

[8] Ibid., p. 89.

[9] Ibid., p. 41.

Hegemonic apples and invisible oranges do not make for commensurable warriors, however, and are far less likely to produce winnable wars for the apples. Martyr-seeking hijackers cannot be defeated by smart bombs, well-trained infantrymen, or nuclear deterrence. So leave them in their inaccessible mountain lairs and anonymous global city hovels and go after rogue state elites in Kabul and Baghdad. Vulnerability trumps culpability. Except that states like Iraq and North Korea are intrinsically more suited to deterrence and containment than to preventive war, so when the doctrine of preventive war is applied to them, it rapidly melts down into something that looks very much like a special case of deterrence—in Tod Lindberg's bold phrase, preemption as "the violent reestablishment of the terms of deterrence."[10]

The Bush administration has admitted as much: at the beginning of 2003, an unnamed senior administration official acknowledged that in the new preemptive strategy "there is also a deterrent element for the bad guys."[11] Faced with a truculent North Korea clearly taking advantage of America's preoccupation with Iraq, a Bush spokesman admitted wanly that the country was not in any case in a position to make good on the threats implicit in its new preventive doctrine, at least when a potential rogue state already had nuclear arms: "I'm not saying we don't have military options," said the flustered aide, "I'm just saying we don't have good ones."[12]

---

[10] Lindberg, "Deterrence and Prevention."

[11] Gordon, "Serving Notice."

[12] David E. Sanger, "Nuclear Anxiety: U.S. Eases Threat on Nuclear Arms for North Korea," *New York Times*, December 30, 2002, p. A1. Leon Fuerth, once Vice-President Gore's foreign policy adviser, noted in an op-ed article that nonaction in the face of North Korea's provocations risked turning President Bush's preventive war rhetoric into "a bluff that is being called," with the outcome that "we are preparing to fight a war with a country that might eventually acquire nuclear weapons, while another country is closing in on the ability to go into mass production" (Leon Fuerth, "Outfoxed by North Korea," *New York Times*, January 1, 2003, p. A15).

The game there quickly became a typical deterrent dance, with North Korea threatening nuclear armament and the United States making noises about isolation, sanctions, and "no blackmail" even as it maintained an aircraft carrier in the region and readied two dozen strategic bombers to fly to Guam, within striking distance of the North Korean nuclear processing facilities at Yongbyon. Following the war in Iraq a Defense Department official (speaking anonymously) actually said, "we are committed in Korea with the types of resources and types of capabilities that we brought to Iraq. And we think that doing that will make our deterrence there much more credible and much stronger."[13]

At this junction, marked by America's actual strategy in both Iraq and North Korea, the differences between preventive war and deterrence grow truly fuzzy. As Charles Krauthammer has correctly pointed out, "the preemption option, if adopted, will serve as a higher form of deterrence. The idea of preemption is to deter states not from using weapons of mass destruction but from acquiring them in the first place."[14] But once it is deployed as a "higher" form of deterrence, a "violent reestablishment of the terms of deterrence," it ceases to be preventive war at all in any strict sense. The real point of preventive war is to intervene boldly in the internal affairs of adversary regimes and terrorist organizations and render redundant the indirect, rational manipulation of behavior that defines containment and deterrence. All deterrence is a kind of agreement to indulge in blackmail. Preventive war eschews all negotiation and hence all blackmail.

When the Israelis bombed the Iraqi nuclear facility at Osirak in

[13] Cited by Thom Shanker, "Lessons From Iraq Include How to Scare Korean Leader," *New York Times*, May 12, 2003, p. A17.

[14] Charles Krauthammer, "The Obsolescence of Deterrence," *Weekly Standard*, December 9, 2002, p. 24.

1981, they rendered moot the question of how to deter Iraq from using or acquiring weapons of mass destruction.[15] That was a true preventive strike. The unexecuted Clinton plan to take out the North Korean nuclear facility at Yongbyon back in 1994 would have done the same thing. Instead, the Clinton administration eventually cut a deal, the Agreed Framework, in which the United States provided North Korea both oil and help in constructing a nuclear power plant at Yongbyon in return for North Korea's pledge not to develop nuclear weapons. Plutonium of the kind that can be weaponized is a by-product of spent uranium (the fuel used in nuclear energy plants), and North Korea agreed to an inspection regime under the auspices of the Atomic Energy Commission to guarantee it would not misuse its access to nuclear energy for such military purposes. Although President Clinton considered the war option, he never let his rhetoric commit him to a military response and so was able to divert the crisis peaceably, averting what could have been a dreadful catastrophe in human terms—if, critics have observed, to the unfortunate end of postponing the crisis into this era, calling for more traditional forms of negotiation, containment, and deterrence.

The slippage from the "new" preventive war doctrine to a much more conventional strategy of negotiation, threats, and carrots representing traditional deterrence-and-containment doctrine has been fairly plain, yet it has been missed by strategists in quest of doctrinal purity. Shortly before the onset of the Iraq war, for example, John J. Mearsheimer and Stephen M. Walt insisted, "The United States faces a clear choice in Iraq: containment or preven-

---

[15] At the time, this preemptive strike was roundly condemned not just by Israel's traditional critics like France but by Britain (which called it "a grave breach of international law") and the Reagan administration.

tive war . . . in fact, war is not necessary."[16] What they missed was that the Bush doctrine had been using preventive war as a policy of containment throughout the months leading to war, and the onset of war signaled the failure of this deterrence/containment policy. President Bush certainly began his war on terrorism with a clearly preventive war doctrine that seemed to offer the choice Mearsheimer and Walt posed. He confirmed the preventive character of his response by calling the terrorists "evil ones" and promising punishment on his own nonnegotiable terms. But as time elapsed and the terrorists proved hard to find, he appeared to slide down the greased slope, calling some fairly arbitrarily chosen selection of sovereign nations an "axis of evil" and thereby altering the moral logic while at the same time raising the global ante. Whose axis of evil? Why not Libya or Cuba, "rogue" enemies of the United States as volatile and despotic as the new axis powers? Why not Vietnam, which had actually defeated the United States but had become a trade partner; or for that matter, why not China, which represents the most powerful communist regime in the world and remains a prominent violator of human rights? It cannot be the connection to terrorism, because North Korea has none and the administration never was able to prove that Iraq was linked to al-Qaeda at all, let alone as closely as were, say, the Pakistani or Saudi intelligence services, or was in a better position to sell its WMD than, say, Chechnya or Kyrgyzstan.

In any case, it is much more difficult to attribute blame in cases of "sponsoring" or "harboring" terrorists than it is to blame terrorists directly. It is far harder to condemn collectives—a state, its gov-

---

[16] John J. Mearsheimer and Stephen M. Walt, "Keeping Saddam Hussein in a Box," *New York Times*, February 2, 2003, sec. 4, p. 15. Mearsheimer and Walt offered a "realist" critique of the Iraq war strategy in the January 2003 issue of *Foreign Policy*, arguing that deterrence alone could have worked perfectly well in Iraq.

ernment, its people, its culture—than individuals. When applied to states, the logic of preventive war runs roughshod over such niceties. In the words of the thoughtful conservative historian Tony Judt, since there seems to be "no clear link between Saddam Hussein and Al Qaeda . . . advocates of a war with Iraq have taken to claiming that such a link can't be excluded, and therefore it should be 'pre-empted.' "[17]

In facing a North Korean crisis it did not want on the way to provoking an Iraqi crisis it did want, the Bush administration had to fumble around to come up with language that saved its preventive war doctrine from total incoherence. Secretary of Defense Rumsfeld explained the difference this way: "the Iraqi regime has thumbed their noses at the United National annually for a good period of time. The situation in North Korea is a fairly recent one . . . [and working diplomatically with Korea's neighbors] seems to me to be a perfectly rational way of proceeding."[18] Even as North Korea threatened at the very end of 2002 to withdraw from the Nuclear Nonproliferation Treaty and to try to entice South Korea (under an untried new president elected with the help of anti-American sentiment) into an all-Korean anti-Americanism, President Bush said simply, "I believe this is not a military showdown, this is a diplomatic showdown."[19] And what is the difference?

The only way to distinguish the cases of the two and preserve the moral rhetoric was to make Iraq out as "more evil" than its axis of evil twin Korea. This is how Secretary of State Colin Powell tried

---

[17] Tony Judt, "The Wrong War at the Wrong Time," *New York Times*, October 20, 2002, sec. 4, p. 11.

[18] Cited by Richard W. Stevenson, "North Korea Begins to Reopen Plant for Processing Uranium," *New York Times*, December 24, 2002, p. A1.

[19] David E. Sanger, "President Makes Case That North Korea Is No Iraq," *New York Times*, January 1, 2003, p. A1.

to make the argument: after all, unlike North Korea, Saddam Hussein has used chemical weapons of mass destruction and in doing so has "demonstrated far more evil intent, seeking to dominate the middle east." Moreover, even if it already had a nuclear weapons capacity, North Korea is "a country that's in desperate condition. What are they going to do with another two or three more nuclear weapons when they're starving, when they have no energy, when they have no economy that's functioning?"[20] A former ambassador to South Korea, Donald Gregg, simply says about the North Koreans: "I don't think these guys are crazy"—presumably not the case with Saddam Hussein, though no clinical psychologists have been asked for their opinions.[21]

On such a tenuous basis, the United States not only tolerated North Korea's extraordinarily provocative actions aimed at developing nuclear weapons but at the end of 2002 allowed North Korean Scud missiles hidden in a cargo ship to be delivered to Yemen (in order not to offend a newly supportive Yemeni government), after they were discovered by a boarding party from a Spanish warship following American intelligence reports. Such embarrassing episodes suggest why idealist exceptionalism with its touching language of morals is an insufficient foundation for protecting American interests. Thirty-seven thousand American troops continue to represent a trip wire in South Korea and are directly under the North Korean gun, if now removed a little further away from the DMZ. Yet the Bush administration was unable to offer any meaningful response at all.

President Bush thus tried to distinguish the case of North Korea, where America was negotiating diplomatically, from the case of

---

[20] Cited in Sanger, "Nuclear Anxiety."

[21] Cited in Howard W. French, "Nuclear Fear as a Wedge," *New York Times*, December 24, 2002, p. A1.

Iraq, where it was hell-bent on war, by declaring: "Hussein is unique, in this sense: he has thumbed his nose at the world for 11 years. . . . He's actually gassed his own people. He has used weapons of mass destruction on neighboring countries and he's used weapons of mass destruction on his own citizenry. He wants to have a nuclear weapon. He has made it very clear he hates the United States and, as importantly, he hates friends of ours."[22] The original animating issue of terrorism had simply vanished from the explanation in favor of more convincing if less relevant reasons for intervention. Yet, taken one by one, even those explanations failed to fully persuade, deriving their conviction from an amassing of claims rather than a preponderance of evidence.[23]

In sliding over the lack of proof for hard linkages between Iraq and terror, the Bush administration also had to contend with the thinness of the evidence demonstrating Iraqi weapons violations of a kind that might make it guilty of planning or supporting terrorist

[22] Quoted in Mike Allen, "Bush Pledges Diplomatic Approach to North Korea," *Washington Post*, October 22, 2002, p. A24.

[23] For example, even the claim that Saddam used chemical agents on his own people, perhaps the most important and least contested of the ancillary charges used by the U.S. government to buttress the generic case against the Iraqi regime as a dangerous and brutal rogue state, has been challenged. Because the terrible Kurdish casualties from chemical agents at Halabja were inflicted during the Iraq-Iran War in the midst of a battle in which both sides may have used chemical agents, there are in fact questions both about whether the Iraqis were using the weapons against the Kurds or against their Iranian opponents and, indeed, even questions about which side employed the toxic agent. See Stephen C. Pelletiere, "A War Crime or an Act of War?," *New York Times*, January 31, 2003, p. A29. Pelletiere's arguments are controversial and have been challenged by credible critics like Kenneth Roth of Human Rights Watch, who holds Iraq alone responsible for the gassing of Kurdish civilians at Halabja. See Roth's letter to the editor, *New York Times*, February 5, 2003. More serious still, it was the United States that provided Iraq with much of its chemical and biological war weapons at a time when America supported Iraq against Iran.

actions. It responded by claiming to have pertinent intelligence contradicting the reports of United Nations inspectors and the views of allies but insisting it could not reveal them for fear of compromising and even endangering sources. It charged the Iraqis with violations explicitly denied by the United Nations' chief inspector, Hans Blix.[24] It fabricated some of its evidence, manipulated and distorted intelligence reports, or simply lied. Aside from raising crucial issues of trust, and without determining ultimate truth, it is clear that applying the logic of preventive war to states is no simple task.

On its face, the case of Afghanistan seems less relevant to this critique. The Taliban government had patently supported terrorist training bases and otherwise evinced their complicity in al-Qaeda's development, if not its actual deeds. Given Taliban ideology, the existence of terrorist training bases and the intimate financial and leadership linkages between the government and al-Qaeda and between Mullah Omar and Osama bin Laden, there could hardly be a more clear-cut case of state sponsorship of terrorism. Although there was room for academic disagreement about the full extent of moral culpability by the Taliban for 9/11, few nations denied that in going after the Taliban, the United States was not merely attacking a nation that harbored terrorists but destroying a regime that was actively complicit in terrorist deeds. Yet even in this seemingly clear case, it turned out that eliminating the Taliban regime failed to eliminate al-Qaeda, which melted away with at least some of its top leadership to fight another day in another place. The logic of sponsorship, even at its persuasive best, goes only in one direction. A state may harbor and sponsor terrorists, but eliminating the state

---

[24] In his State of the Union address, President Bush contended that the old warheads discovered by inspectors on January 16, 2003, were proof of Saddam's plans to use chemical and biological agents; but Blix reported that "no trace" of chemical or biological elements had been found in the warheads (or anywhere else, for that matter).

cannot and will not eliminate the terrorists. They receive support but are not dependent on it or those who give it. Terrorists are often compared to cancerous tumors that destroy themselves when they destroy their hosts, but they are actually much more like mobile parasites who live in host bodies but can move from host to host as they infect and destroy the systems off which they live. The Taliban are gone, al-Qaeda lives. The era of Saddam Hussein is over, the era of Jihad against America is just getting under way.

New host states abound. They include dozens of corrupt and undemocratic regimes, numerous governments that are weak and unstable, and more than a few Third World societies marginalized by globalization and hostile to America. They also include authoritarian as well as protodemocratic regimes that are allies and friends of America, such as Egypt, Yemen, Morocco, Saudi Arabia, and Pakistan, all of whom have "harbored" and currently harbor terrorists—if sometimes inadvertently. When does "helping" a "friend" like Indonesia or the Philippines make war on terrorism turn into an American war on the friend? Over 1,700 American combat commando forces stand ready to "assist" Philippine President Arroyo disrupt and destroy an estimated 250 members of the extremist group Abu Sayyaf; but it turns out the Philippine government has hesitated in letting them in.

The comparative threat posed by particular states (whether they are "rogue states," terrorist "sponsors," or merely unfriendly) to the United States and other nations needs to be assessed by common standards that are clear and empirically based so that they can be recognized by international bodies like the UN Security Council and the International Criminal Court. The mere presence of an unstable or despotic regime (definitive of dozens of nations) is not enough. The key criteria relate not to the character, stability, democracy, or legitimacy of the state but to the nature of its connections with terrorism. The mere presence of terrorists on a state's territory is obviously insufficient, since terrorists are to be found in

Canada, England, Germany, the United States, and many other Western nations. Indeed, if terrorists flourish in unstable societies, they also do well, and are far harder to detect, in open societies. In the past, Ireland (the IRA), Italy and Germany (the Red Brigades), Spain (the Basque region), Cambodia, and (ex-Soviet) Georgia were among the many countries thought to be sources of international terrorism. American far-right-wing militia groups and other paramilitary organizations have not only committed terrorist acts in the United States but have sought alliances with neofascists in Germany and elsewhere, often utilizing the same international technologies such as the World Wide Web favored by better known terrorist networks.[25] The State Department's official list of terrorist organizations and states that sponsor terrorism reads quite differently than President Bush's shorthand axis of evil roster—it includes Cuba, Sudan, and Syria, as well as twenty-eight "foreign terrorist organizations" including Aum Shinrikyo, Kach, the Tamil Liberation Tigers, the Basque ETA, the Shining Path, and the Tupac Amaru Revolutionary Movement.[26] Just as there are legal criteria by which courts can identify particular crimes as felonious, capital, and so on, there is a need for legal criteria by which collective security bodies can identify state acts as culpable for or complicit in terrorist criminality. Had such criteria been available in judging Iraq, the United States either would have been able to gain wider support for its war or would have had to proceed (if it chose to do so) in explicit violation of the law.

[25] For documentation, see the reports of the Southern Poverty Law Center (at www.splcenter.org).

[26] The distinction between national and international terrorists is, of course, slippery and problematic for those who wish to strike preemptively against "international" terrorism. Clearly even counterterrorist preventive war must be conducted with extreme caution.

Such criteria aside, issues of risk, of certainty and uncertainty, of responsibility and blame clearly become extremely fluid in the slippery logic of preventive war. States make poor candidates for preventive war because they are part of an international system defined by sovereignty and (under the United Nations Charter) by the mutual obligation to avoid war except when it can be justified by self-defense or a threat so imminent that preemption can be understood as a kind of anticipatory self-defense.

When preventive war is applied to states, all of the issues of rationality, predictability, and certainty that afflict traditional doctrines of deterrence and containment reappear. Thus, the United States is involved in a guessing game about intentions, motivations, and rationality in North Korea that is not so very different from the guessing games in which it was involved in dealing with the Soviet Union in the era of the Cold War—and in which it continues to be engaged today (wholly apart from terrorism) with, say, China and Cuba. Perhaps Condoleezza Rice, who spent many years as a Sovietologist, has come less far from her academic origins than she supposes in postulating a "new" doctrine of preventive war. The tendency to see in Saddam a figure who administration officials insist reminded them of Stalin certainly did less to vilify Saddam than to rationalize reintroducing by the back door the deterrence strategies that had been so publicly thrown off the front porch. While some will insist the deterrence option was never seriously embraced by the president, its logic was very much in play in Iraq and could have actually compelled Bush to pursue containment— had Saddam fully complied with every demand.

Prior to the American invasion, preventive war was applied in Iraq the way nuclear deterrence was applied to the Soviet Union: not "you're done for, it's over, whatever you do now, you will be attacked and disarmed" but rather "unless you cooperate with United Nations inspectors, unless you show you are disarmed or take visible steps to disarm yourself, unless you change your regime or if not your regime your military ambitions, we will disarm you." This is containment, deterrence, a use of potential force to effect desired changes in an opponent's behavior. However tough, and while it failed finally as deterrence, it was deployed as a form of negotiating with the enemy in precisely the way the president pledged he would not negotiate with terrorists. However savvy, it allows the opponent a crucial role in determining the outcome. Sincere or not, President Bush said over and over again that whether or not there was war would be up to Saddam Hussein and Saddam Hussein alone. He needed only to comply fully with Resolution 1441 (something that not even those who opposed American intervention thought he had done).

The message of the war on terrorism, however, was very different: it was "we will find you, interdict you, destroy you. Period. Nothing depends on you." True preventive war needs no United Nations resolutions and demands no justifications. "You began it," President Bush told the terrorists, "we will finish it." The message to Iraq, however, was: "unless you disarm, we will disarm you." That's not a declaration, that's a threat. Everything depends on the adversary. This is not preventive war but the *threat* of preventive war used as a tool in the kitbag of containment and deterrence. So much for the doctrine of containment "not holding water" anymore.

With both Iraq and North Korea, there have been implicit state-to-state negotiations with a schedule of negotiable prices being set for a variety of desired outcomes. The same is true for Syria and Iran today. It turned out that even regime change in Baghdad, initially a sine qua non of American restraint, was negotiable. If Saddam complied fully with Resolution 1441, this would, America declared, be understood as regime change. Treating Iraq and North Korea like states with interests rather than like stateless terrorists, the United States turned the "new" preventive war doctrine back into the "old" deterrence and containment doctrine.

In fact, the preventive war strategy in Iraq, at its best, looked a lot like a powerful bluff whose credibility was being underwritten day by day through a variety of deterrent means: through a massive buildup of arms in the region, through the clarity with which the administration issued threats and warnings; and through its apparent readiness to act unilaterally if it could not persuade the UN or its allies to participate. "Multilateralism cannot become an excuse for inaction," said a determined Colin Powell before the delegates at the 2003 World Economic Forum in Davos. "We continue to reserve our sovereign right to take military action against Iraq alone or in a coalition of the willing."[27] Preventive war here is meant to incentivize action on the other side precisely in order to prevent having to implement preventive war. It is deterrence with the ante raised. It stretches the subjunctive logic of "if you don't do X, then we will do Y" to the breaking point. Far from freeing itself from the paradoxes and contradictions of deterrence, however, it enhances their troublesome impact—even as it creates new problems of seeming illegality, unilateralism, and exceptionalist one-sidedness. It turns the passive or reactive deterrence of the Cold War into an aggressive form of "active deterrence" that others see as bullying.

Containment against the Soviets invoked a more conventional deterrent logic: "We know you have the capacity to launch a first nuclear strike against us, or to launch a conventional war in Europe on the (false) belief we will not risk a nuclear exchange by responding. So we are here to tell you, 'don't!' For we will launch a counterstrike more devastating than any first strike you may deliver;

---

[27] Secretary of State Colin Powell, speech to the World Economic Forum, Davos, Switzerland, as reported in "Powell on Iraq: 'We Reserve Our Right to Take Military Action,'" *New York Times*, January 27, 2003, p. A8.

and if you strike conventionally and overwhelm our conventional defenses, we reserve all our options, including the nuclear option. The proof: we have not only put American troops on the eastern front as a 'trip wire,' we have placed nuclear weapons in that theater."

When preventive war is reduced to a tactic of active deterrence, it speaks the same general language but with a much stronger rhetoric of intimidation—immersed, however, in a much weaker subjunctive logic. This logic avers: "We think you may be planning an attack against us, or that your ideology suggests you would if you could; or if you are telling the truth (we don't think you are) and you don't yet have weapons capable of hurting us, we suspect you may be planning to acquire such weapons that would allow you to attack the United States or its friends, if you wanted to, which we think you do, and even if you don't, you would have the power to turn over these weapons to terrorists, which we believe you might. . . ." Such logic is not the "no negotiation, no deals" logic of real preventive war, but it is not quite the tacit but sure logic of passive deterrence either. Because its credibility is grounded in preemptive action rather than reaction and insists that its enemy must *do something* (disarm, comply with inspections, change regimes) rather than *desist from doing something* (don't attack, don't first strike), it complicates the already tortured logic of deterrence.

Preemption as threat lacks the force of simple preemption ("we're going in no matter what!") without achieving the virtue of passive deterrence ("as long as you do nothing, we will do nothing"). Back in the Cold War years, mutual assured destruction deterred each side from a first strike by guaranteeing a devastating counterstrike by the aggressed-against party. But the government of Iraq was not told: "If you use chemical or biological weapons in any war that threatens us or our allies, you will risk massive retaliation by the United States, including possible nuclear retaliation."

That was in fact the actual message the first Bush administration delivered to Saddam Hussein during the Kuwait war, when it feared the Iraqis might in desperation use its biochemical weapons against the allied counter-attack following the Iraqi invasion of Kuwait. *That* was traditional deterrence and containment. But prior to invasion, Iraq was told by the second Bush administration to take specific actions, to do rather than to desist. Show us the weapons of mass destruction America says you have, or prove definitively you do not have them (and America will tell you what constitutes definitive proof) or you will be destroyed. This is "active deterrence." Unlike the traditional version, it makes the deterring party the aggressor. It demands that Iraq as a sovereign state (however tyrannical and repellent its regime) accommodate its own right to develop weapons and tactics of self-defense to the perceived threat such weapons and tactics evoke in the United States. It thus asks the world to legitimate the right of the stronger, who claims to be morally superior, to intimidate the weaker, who is deemed morally inferior.

In this sense the application of preventive war as an active deterrent threat succeeds only by failing. And fails when it succeeds. That is to say, it works as a deterrent only when it fails as preventive war: when prevention is threatened but not actually implemented. And it works as preventive war (a preventive strike is launched) only by failing as deterrence: as when the Iraqi regime was not intimidated into compliance by the threat of war and so was attacked. This paradoxical logic of preventive war as deterrence was aptly captured just before war with Iraq began in a *New York Times* editorial observing, "If the Bush administration's aim is to keep military pressure on Mr. Hussein to encourage him to cooperate more fully with the inspectors or accept a diplomatic deal, the results could be constructive. But if Washington is actually planning an early military strike in the weeks just ahead, either on its own or with only British support, it should reconsider."[28] In other words, it's fine to threaten preventive war to prevent war (though this means preventive war "failed" in that it was not necessary!) as long as you don't actually go to war (which would mean deterrence failed since it did not deter war!) But of course you can't effectively threaten to go to war without being fully and believably ready to go to war, and the final proof for the credibility of the threat is that you actually go to war.

Some of the paradoxes of preventive war applied as a deterrent strategy rest on the paradoxes of deterrence itself. There is a certain irony in the nostalgia liberal critics of President Bush seem to feel for the policies of containment and deterrence of the Cold War era, as if many of these same liberals were not once harsh critics of deterrence strategy, and as if those policies were without extraordinary risks of their own, which those same critics once made a living fuming about. As Max Boot has acknowledged, the reality behind containment was "a good deal more sordid" that today's liberal enthusiasts remember: "it meant support for the Greek colonels, the Argentine generals, the shah, Pinochet, Marcos, Somoza, and other unsavory characters who were in 'our' camp. It meant helping to overthrow . . . Mossadegh in Iran, Arbenz in Guatemala and Allende in Chile . . . [and] it meant major war against North Korea and North Vietnam . . . [and] invasions of the Dominican Republic and Grenada."[29]

The truth is the assumptions that underlie the new preventive

---

[28] Editorial, "Lighting the Fuse in Iraq," *New York Times*, January 22, 2003, p. A20.

[29] Max Boot, "Look Who Likes Deterrence Now," *Weekly Standard*, November 11, 2002, p. 27. As Boot notes, gloatingly but also accurately, "The Left's enthusiasm for containment and deterrence was, to put it mildly, a lot harder to detect during the Cold War."

war strategy are rooted in the same rationalistic strategic thinking that produced both the balance of terror and its critics; that produced the debates over rationality, predictability, and certainty that led many strategic thinkers to doubt the wisdom of deterrence. The defects that made the strategy of containment and passive deterrence dicey during the Cold War (and that lead some today to think of preventive war as an alternative) make a contemporary strategy of preventive war and active deterrence disastrous today. Deterrence worked but it worked as much through good luck as good design, and did so at the risk of human survival.

Good fortune had something to do with how the United States and the Soviet Union survived the paradoxical credibility issues that have always made deterrence into something resembling a game of global chicken. Deterrence can only work by making *credible* threats, and the credibility of threats rests entirely on the adversary's belief that the nation trying to deter it *will* act as it threatens to, even if that means mutual annihilation. To maximize credibility is to maximize the perceived likelihood (perception is everything!) of a swift and unambiguous and certain carrying out of the deterrent promise. Just weeks before the conflict in Iraq began, Prime Minister Blair gave to a suspicious House of Commons the classic argument for not backing down in the game of global chicken: "Show weakness now," he explained, "and no one will ever believe us when we try to show strength in the future."[30] In the case of the Cold War, the stakes were even higher.

The need for credibility posed a problem then as it does now: the actual execution of a nuclear counterstrike annihilating the Soviets, after the United States was destroyed in a first strike, would only compound the lunatic mayhem of the initial strike. But

[30] Cited by Warren Hoge, "Blair, Despite a Dubious Public, Sticks to a Firm Stance on Iraq," *New York Times*, February 4, 2003, p. A12.

unless both sides believed the other side would proceed to the mutual assured destruction of a counterstrike, even at the risk of nuclear Armageddon, deterrence would not work and the threat of war would be increased. Only by making the threat of a devastating potential war counterstrike ironclad, could the risk of actual war be reduced. Indeed, the more sensitive the trigger and more devastating the consequences, the more effective deterrence would be—and the more catastrophic the consequences of its failure would be. The threat of massive retaliation "worked" in the Cold War because neither side dared test the lunatic logic on which it rested. Its credibility and hence its rationality rested on its incredibility and its irrationality: "You mean if hundreds of millions of innocent Americans were slaughtered in a Soviet strike, America would slaughter hundreds of millions of innocent Russians, even though that would do nothing to save America?!" Yes, the more irrational the outcome, the more credible the threat.

The ultimate logic of MAD (you destroy my country, I'll destroy yours) was the literally mad "doomsday machine"—a hypothetical device, proposed by caustic critics of MAD, that would "deter" nuclear aggressors by wiring the earth with sensors that triggered a whole-earth nuclear meltdown in response to any nuclear weapon being set off. Mutual assured destruction's incredibility was in truth the secret to its credibility, and was made easier to buy into by the moralism that underlay Cold War rhetoric. Communism was a "totalitarian" ideology, the Soviet Union an "evil empire," so that extreme measures were necessary. Nonetheless, MAD could not be supported by just war doctrine.[31] It promised more than a killing

---

[31] The U.S. Conference of Catholic Bishops regarded it as a violation of "just war theory," arguing that "it is not morally acceptable to intend to kill the innocent as part of a strategy of deterring nuclear war" ("The Challenge of Peace: God's Promise and Our Response," pastoral letter, May 3, 1983, ¶ 178).

of innocents: it promised to kill everyone as a way to stop the enemy from killing anyone.

From this perspective on deterrence, even when "the good guys" are deploying the strategy, it is not hard to understand why some prudent observers such as the eminent political psychologist Robert Jay Lifton find a certain nutty parallelism today in the terrorists' nihilism and the American vision of appropriate forms of preventive interdiction. As Lifton suggests, Hamas and others use "apocalyptic violence . . . aimed at large-scale destruction and to renew the world spirit . . . but you also have this here in the U.S. among those who use the threat of terror to justify world domination militarily."[32]

Pax Americana, resting on both novel preventive war strategy and traditional deterrence doctrines, pays a terrible price, even if it succeeds in the short term (I am arguing it cannot succeed long term). For Lifton, as in the case of MAD, these oppositional groups "act in concert" as they righteously "denounce one another." I do not share Lifton's fear that "a war on terror, without limits on time or place, brings us one step closer to the use of apocalyptic violence." I worry rather that transferring the appropriate certainties of a necessary preventive war against terrorism to the far less certain terrain of "active deterrence" against sovereign states will return us to the grave risks of the Cold War era, compounded by nonstate terrorist activities. As Charles Krauthammer points out, "even under the best of circumstances, deterrence was psychologically debilitating, inherently unstable, and highly dangerous. To voluntarily choose it as the principle on which to rest our safety in this era of weapons of mass destruction is sheer folly."[33] Surely this is no less true today than it was in the Cold War.

---

[32] Quoted in Chris Hedges, "A Skeptic About Wars Intended to Stamp Out Evil," *New York Times*, January 14, 2003, p. B3.

[33] Krauthammer, "Obsolesence of Deterrence."

Both deterrent and preemptive war doctrine often seem to rest on an assumption of perfect human rationality: on the belief that there is a kind of public schedule of goods and bads, pains and pleasures, penalties and incentives that are universal and will operate without regard to culture, time, or ideology. Carrots and sticks are often the whole of American national security strategy, and less changed after 9/11 than one might have expected. "Money talked in Afghanistan," enthused an antiterrorism special operations chief in the early days of the war in Afghanistan. "Warlords or sub-commanders with dozens or hundreds of fighters could be bought off for as little as 50K in cash. . . . If we do this right, we can buy off a lot more of the Taliban than we have to kill."[34] On the same principle (and with equally little success), the United States offered a $25 million reward for Osama bin Laden. More than eighteen months later he was still at large, with some Americans expressing disbelief that no one had stepped up to collect.

This reliance on carrots and sticks is still another side of the Hobbesian philosophy from which social-contract doctrine is derived: what moral philosophers call psychological hedonism. Psychological hedonism (a component of classical utilitarian theory) was perfected a century and a half after Hobbes by that brilliant and obsessive student of human rationality Jeremy Bentham. Bentham understood human reason as a kind of instrument of and slave to human passions—a calculating machine by which we reckon the likely impact of behaviors we may engage in, based on their probability of producing either pain or pleasure in us.

Whole systems of human learning and political legislation are built on this simple premise. Our supposedly perfect rationality arises out of and is merely a servant of our common passions and needs, which means all men and women everywhere engage in the

[34] Woodward's reconstruction of the comments, *Bush at War*, p. 194.

same calculations, whether they are American strategic planners, Viet Cong guerrillas, Iraqi generals, or al-Qaeda terrorists. They are all potentially subject to manipulation by rewards and sanctions, big bucks and big bombs.[35]

For each example suggesting that human experience is uniform and instrumentally rationalistic and calculating, that incentives and sanctions can work, that deterrence makes sense, there is a counterexample—for instance, the onset of World War I despite a century of "concert of nations" diplomacy that was supposed to assure such a thing could not happen (see *The Guns of August*, Barbara Tuchman's still powerful account of the misbegotten onset of that war to end all wars). The Vietnam War itself is perhaps the most persuasive counterexample of the limits of rationality. The American bombing of the North in the name of raising the stakes so high that the North Vietnamese government would lose interest in the civil war in the South, far from deterring it, seemed to steel its will and focus its resistance. Saddam Hussein's assault on Kuwait, despite the overwhelming power of his prospective enemies, offers another counterexample. There is the ongoing "success" of suicide bombing by Palestinian terrorists in Israel despite a preventive war policy that aspires to deter such behavior by compelling perpetrators to forfeit their families' homes and the collective security and liberty of the larger Palestinian community, which is forced to pay a collective price for their zealotry. The Sharon government believes (or once believed) no "rational" pro-terrorist government or the

---

[35] Jeremy Bentham, *Principles of Morals and Legislation* (1780), chap. 1. In Bentham's famous opening, "Nature has placed mankind under the governance of two sovereign masters, pain and pleasure. It is for them alone to point out what we ought to do, as well as to determine what we shall do. . . . They govern us in all we do, in all we say, in all we think. . . . In words a man may pretend to abjure their empire: but in reality he will remain subject to it all the while."

terrorists themselves could hold out against such overwhelming preventive/deterrent force. The Palestinians turn out not to share this instrumental understanding of what is rational, however.

Why then does deterrence fail? Because human beings are not identical rational calculating machines with the same glossary of needs, wants, and passions. Because different cultures treat pain and pleasure in different ways. Because in many ideologies (including some versions of our own), staying alive is not the ultimate reward and death is not the ultimate sanction. "Give me liberty or give me death" was once an American aphorism that defeated a superior British army unable to vanquish the "irrationality" of such a stance. Modern deterrence theory makes the mistakes for which the wise John Stuart Mill criticized Jeremy Bentham's "felicific calculus." Bentham posited a rationality in men so perfect that it could actually be reckoned out mathematically in terms of specifiable characteristics of human behavior.[36] In doing so, Mill notes, Bentham conceives man exclusively as a passion-driven calculating machine—"a being susceptible of pleasures and pains, and governed in all his conduct partly by the different modifications of self-interest, and the passions commonly classed as selfish. . . . And here Bentham's conception of human nature stops. . . . Man is never recognized by him as a being capable of pursuing spiritual perfection as an end; of desiring, for its own sake, the conformity of his own character to his standard of excellence, without hope of good or fear of evil from other source than his own inward consciousness."[37]

---

[36] Bentham has proposed in his *Introduction to the Principles of Morals and Legislation* that human behavior rested on a calculation about the likely pain or pleasure to result from the duration, propinquity, intensity, and certainty of each act.

[37] J. S. Mill, "On Bentham," in G. Himmelfarb, *Essays on Politics and Culture* (New York: Doubleday Anchor, 1963), p. 97. Originally published in *London and Westminister Review*, August 1838.

Strategic planners from ancient Greece through the Cold War down into the age of terror have demonstrated a Bethamite narrowness in their psychic conception of their enemies. King Creon of ancient Thebes thought he could threaten or bribe Antigone into compliance with his authority, but Antigone heeded the voice of gods not men. The British believed their eighteenth-century military machine would intimidate the poorly trained, badly armed American militiamen arrayed against them into submission. But the Americans had a deeper faith in their cause. Human beings are not psychic or moral clones, and it is simply not the case that "every man can be bought" or that it's just a matter of finding his price. Conscience, whether attuned to high moral righteousness or to an old-fashioned nationalism or fanatic religious dogmatism that resists every invader, even when it comes in liberty's name, resists rational calculations and strategic intimidation. However often such policies succeed in particular cases, they often fail in the long term. Saddam's refusal to acquiesce to certain defeat for his country and certain death or exile for himself was certainly "irrational" in the Benthamite sense, and the determination of thousands to fight to the bitter end in his sullied name was even more so. But irrationality is probably a better bet than rationality in thinking about war, whether as a deterrent or as prevention, which means unpredictability is war's most important characteristic.

Irrationality means unpredictability: the incapacity, even for the party that holds all the cards and so is in a position of unrivaled power, to know how its behavior and utterances will play out in an opponent's individual or collective psyche. War always raises the stakes for the unexpected to happen and the unforeseen to occur. Hence Harry Truman's dictum, born of bitter experience, that war cannot buy the peace in whose name it is usually conducted. From the success against Nazi Germany came the long Cold War struggle against the Soviet Union. From the defeat of the Soviets has come the strange new war against terrorism. From the defeat of Saddam has come anarchy, disorder, bitterness, and disappointment; perhaps one day democracy, perhaps not. Indeed, because certainty about consequences and outcomes grow dimmer as time horizons become more remote, the likely impact of a given behavior on an adversary—even an adversary sharing the same cultural values and background—cannot always be determined. Al-Qaeda's leaders said they thought the United States was weak and its citizens afraid to die fighting foreign wars in distant lands. That they were wrong only shows the power of miscalculation to lead to untoward consequences.

Those who believe they can fully control the course of human events under any circumstances, let alone under fear's sway or the anarchy of war, are not merely delusional but likely to be the first victims of their hubris. The French Revolution started as a reform movement among aristocrats hoping to increase their leverage on the monarchy and ended by destroying both the aristocracy and the monarchy. No wonder the French are given to muttering *l'inattendu toujours arrive*: in a country as intimate with war and revolution as France, the unexpected always *does* seem to happen. For as Winston Churchill somberly noted, once embarked "on the strange voyage" of war, "the statesman who yields to [its] fever must realize that once the signal is given, he is no longer the master of policy but the slave of unforeseeable and uncontrollable events." The fragility of human understanding and the limits of human capacity are never far from view. Just weeks prior to the American invasion of Iraq, the space shuttle *Columbia* disintegrated as it reentered earth's atmosphere following a sixteen-day mission in orbit. The day after the accident, reporting that the president saw in the *Columbia* catastrophe a "tragedy that has touched the lives of the American people and as a reminder of the risks of space flight," White House Press Secretary Ari Fleischer rushed to add that Bush did "not see it as connected to other events around the world."[38] In the president's self-certainty there is a hint of Icarus, of lessons unlearned that invite disaster.

George W. Bush has acknowledged the uncertainty of war: he told Bob Woodward that he had chosen advisers experienced in war who had "been in situations where the plan didn't happen the way it was planned."[39] But there has been little hint of humility in his decision making. His insight into indeterminacy seems to have impacted little on his actions. His unphilosophical temperament makes him unreceptive to subtlety and complexity but quick to move toward decisions; it allows him to move swiftly from decisions to their execution and leaves him obstinate in staying the course once decisions are taken. These are useful qualities in fighting wars imposed on the United States by others but qualities too likely to lead him to impose war on others when alternatives may still be available. In the war on terrorism, started by others, these qualities put "calcium in the backbone" of his administration, as he himself has said. But in pursuing solutions to the complex situations in the Middle East and East Asia they risk ossifying the administration's backbone, rendering it rigid and inflexible.

A dozen years ago, a more sober observer of the costs of a possible invasion of Iraq and overthrow of its regime following the Kuwait war warned:

> If you're going to go in and try to topple Saddam Hussein, you
> have to go to Baghdad. Once you've got Baghdad, it's not clear

---

[38] Cited by Richard W. Stevenson, "Loss of the Shuttle: The President," *New York Times*, February 3, 2003, p. A1.

[39] Woodward, *Bush at War*, p. 136.

what you do with it. It's not clear what kind of government you would put in place of the one that's currently there now. It is going to be a Shia regime, a Sunni regime or a Kurdish regime? Or one that tilts toward the Baathists, or one that tilts toward the Islamic fundamentalists? How much credibility is that government going to have if it's set up by the United States military when it's there? How long does the United States military have to stay to protect the people that sign on for that government, and what happens to it once we leave?"[40]

The sober realist of that era was then–secretary of defense Dick Cheney, who ought to be consulted about the uncertainty that attends war and its outcomes in regions as complex as the Middle East by current Vice-President Dick Cheney as he surveys the wreckage of Saddam Hussein's Baghdad.

As the culture is more alien, the issues grow more complex, the values more distinctive, and the relevant time horizons more variable. No mere calculation of incentives and penalties, no counting up of strategic assets or military resources are reliable predictors of outcomes. Prior to the Iraq war, Saddam appeared to pay far too little attention to the high-octane moral rhetoric of the Bush administration that was intended especially for him, while the North Korean leadership was paying far too much attention, insisting America must be planning an aggression against its regime. A preventive war doctrine misapplied to one state with a recklessly public rhetoric not only failed to deter its primary target, putting America at war with Iraq rather than with terrorism, but it incensed a hostile "bystander" regime, raising the risks of a wholly

[40] Patrick E. Tyler, "After the War: U.S. Juggling Iraq Policy," *New York Times*, April 13, 1991, sec. 1, p. 5.

unwanted war with it—a war that, if it comes, is also unlikely to seriously impact the real war on terrorism.

In this regard, the pure preventive doctrine is even worse than its deterrent version. For while in the deterrence mode, preventive war merely reserves the right to a preventive strike as a "sovereign right" (Colin Powell at Davos in 2003), in the pure preemptive mode it actually implements that right, waving off possible deterrent effects and striking without regard for the opponent's reactions. It pays all of the heavy costs of entering into a war as an initiator without being able to assure that the variable and wholly uncertain benefits of outcomes offset these costs, even by the limited measure of its own rationalistic calculus. That would appear to be the thrust of Dick Cheney's prudent 1991 warning against taking Baghdad. Preemptive war pays the certain costs of war without assuring the indeterminate spoils of peace. Its subjunctive logic means that it enters the fray on the basis of a series of conditionals which, if they fail to pan out, can make war a very bad bargain at best.

In response to 9/11, inaction was rightly deemed to be more costly than action, quite literally "suicidal" (as the President said in ordering the invasion of Iraq). Except that Iraq was neither the perpetrator of 9/11 nor a demonstrable threat to the United States eighteen months later. No Iraqi soldier had stepped foot out of Iraq since the Republican Guard was driven from Kuwait in 1991, no Iraqi agent had been discovered fomenting terror anywhere in the world, no WMD were found either by UN inspectors before the war or by U.S. occupiers after the war (at least in the first several months). Yet with a preventive war against terrorism turned toward Baghdad, high costs were paid up front (the United Nations alienated; allies angered; Muslims incensed; American casualties suffered; Iraqi civilians killed; oil production slowed; museums,

libraries, and universities pillaged; high war costs paid) for benefits
that may or may not be forthcoming (democracy? other rogue
states intimidated? terrorists stymied? [not in Riyadh or
Casablanca!]). Iraq has been a distraction from other strategic
goals, which include nurturing America's alliances, strengthening
the United Nations, preventing Iran, Syria, and North Korea from
obtaining the nuclear weapons they clearly have the potential to
develop, and most important, pursuing the war on the real (if invisible) terrorists who continue to be active and effective. These costs
all represent the very high price being paid for uncertain long-term
benefits.

When the war on terrorism is understood as a traditional war of
self-defense, even if fought by untraditional means against unconventional (nonstate) enemies who have committed nonconven-
tional forms of aggression, the remedy is always worth the cost,
because the defender can calculate the damage already done to it
by its enemy's aggression. But with a truly preventive war in the
absence of overt aggression by an enemy, the opposite is true: the
costs are certain, the benefits indeterminate.

History unfolds under the sway of what Hegel called the "cunning of reason" in ways no free agent may have intended or wished
for. America yesterday so often prepared the soil in which America's enemies today grow strong. Many of Iraq's weapons, including
anthrax, were acquired with the direct support of the United States
and used with the tacit consent of the United States at a time when
our enmity to Iran made our enemy's enemy (Iraq) our friend.
(Donald Rumsfeld visited with Saddam Hussein in the early 1980s
during the period when Saddam was deploying these weapons.)
America helped arm and support the Muhajadeen against the
Soviet occupation of Afghanistan in the 1980s and a decade later
reaped the reward of the Taliban and their support for al-Qaeda.

America was defeated by North Vietnam but now counts the government there as a trading partner and, at least, a neutral in its current quarrels. What was once the world's most notorious rogue state, Qaddafi's Libya, now cooperates with the United States in the war on terrorism and chairs the United Nations Human Rights Commission (if not exactly as a consequence of American support). Gerry Adams, the infamous IRA's political chief, now takes meetings with world leaders.

Meanwhile Cuba, a longtime target of America sanctions, armed interdiction, assassination, and perduring hostility, as well as the agent that brought the United States close to a nuclear showdown with the Soviet Union, remains under the control of Fidel Castro and his militant brand of communism long after the Soviet Union has vanished. Chased from Somalia by a bloodthirsty warlord and betrayed in Sudan by a hostile government, the United States nonetheless counts the Horn of Africa today as one of the less troublesome parts of the world, at least for it. Even in Sudan, a terrorist hot spot a few years ago, the government extended at least some cooperation on seeking out terrorists in the period after 9/11.

On the other hand, Egypt, the beneficiary of more American largesse than any nation in the world other than Israel, and Saudi Arabia, America's most important and closest oil ally, have become sources of doubt and mistrust. With its support for militant Wahhabi Islam, its repressive monarchy, and its disgruntled citizens' role in terrorist activities outside (and now inside) the kingdom, Saudi Arabia may play a more significant covert role in the rise of al-Qaeda than any member of the axis of evil.[41] Pakistan, America's

---

[41] See, for example, Dore Gold's *Hatred's Kingdom: How Saudi Arabia Supports the New Global Terrorism* (Washington, D.C.: Regnery Publishing, 2003).

ally, is a more likely source of weapons of mass destruction for terrorists than Iraq, and though it has a friendly president, is troubled by a population deeply suspicious of America. It is teeming with refugees from the Afghanistan war whose children are being educated in fundamentalist madrasahs, and who see in the United States their bitterest enemy. Scavenging in a dump, a twenty-two-year-old Afghan refugee from America's liberation war there replied to an American reporter who had asked him what he thought of the Americans: "If I were the ruler of the world, I would kill them all."[42] Thus does the cunning of reason make fools of those who deem their own war plans foolproof and the wish of others for peace foolish.

In a democracy, doubts and humility about how much we can know for certain must be shared with the citizenry. After all, the recognition that I might be wrong and my opponent right is at the very heart of the democratic faith. In a world of certain knowledge, Platonic philosophers—knowers of the Truth—rule; in a world without certain knowledge, doubt offers a persuasive brief for democracy: truth, if such there be, may belong only to a few; error belongs to us all. Including our leaders.

Reading history with democratic doubt and an eye for the logic of unintended consequences has clear policy consequences. It encourages policies that minimize taking major risks up front for uncertain rewards down the line. Preventive war necessitates the analysis of causal chains and concatenations of events far less certain and far more subject to whim and fortune than the kinds of analysis associated with traditional deterrence—which were complicated and dangerous enough in their own right. It is hence far riskier. As Senator Jay Rockefeller said in commenting on the

---

[42] David Rohde, "A Dead End for Afghan Children Adrift in Pakistan," *New York Times*, March 7, 2003, p. A3.

WMD intelligence failures in Iraq, "If you're going to have a doctrine of pre-emption, then you sure as heck better have pluperfect intelligence."[43]

Bush's uneven approach to uncertainty and risk was evident at a November 7, 2002, news conference where he was at pains both to reassure America that war was not inevitable and to assure Saddam that it was. He begins with a clarity mirroring his steely will: "We have an obligation to lead. . . . And I intend to assume that obligation to make the world more peaceful." Good: preventive war is intended as a deterrent to actual war. But: "Listen, there's risk in all action we take. But the risk of inaction is not a choice as far as I'm concerned. The inaction creates more risk than doing our duty to make the world more peaceful." Not quite as clear, but social scientists would agree that decisions not to act, so-called non-decisions, are actually decisions as well, and they can have consequences. Yet as the president's logic grows subjunctive, the would-be picture he is trying to draw grows blurry: "Obviously I weighed all the consequences," he assures his anxious listeners, as if they might not believe the comment about the risk of inaction. Nevertheless, he still hopes "we can do this peacefully" and is quick to add "don't get me wrong . . . if the world were to collectively come together to do so [resolve things peacefully] and to put pressure on Saddam Hussein and convince him to disarm, there's a chance he may decide to do that." As he concludes, he sinks into a morass of subjunctive incoherence: "And war is not my first choice, don't get, you know, it's my last choice. But nevertheless it is a, it is an option in order to make the world a more peaceful place."[44]

[43] Quoted in John Diamond and Bill Nichols, "Bush's War Doctrine Questioned," *USA Today*, June 6, 2003, p. A8.

[44] Quoted in "Excerpts from News Conference: Imagine 'Hussein and Nuclear Weapons,'" *New York Times*, November 8, 2002, p. A24.

The syntax here reflected not simply the president's occasional awkwardness with words but the far deeper awkwardness of preventive war's logic as a tool of deterrence. In Iraq, if it was even actually intended as such, it failed. Why? In part, because the circle cannot be closed: what is required is a threat so intimidating that it nullifies the peril. Yet there is the very real risk that making the threat fully credible removes all possibility of rational response by the targeted enemy, who sees itself confronting not a very forceful negotiation (calculated to inspire a change) but a fait accompli in which nothing it does is relevant—freeing it to do as it pleases (increasing the peril!) prior to being annihilated. This is what transpired in Iraq. The escalating logic led the United States prior to the war to refuse to rule out the use of nuclear weapons in Iraq, although banning the development and use of such weapons was at the heart of America's own incursion.[45]

The logic of preventive war is meant to deter adversaries from hostility. Instead, it provokes them to it. America uses harsh moralizing words justifying preemptive interdiction to subdue adversaries and is surprised to find that they are aroused. Paradoxically it is the very self-righteousness that convinces Americans they would not act unless they had to that convinces America's enemies America will act even if it has no reason.

Yet surely a nation committed to the principle that war must always be justified, that it is superior to others in its pursuit of virtue, must meet a very high standard in going to war. Democra-

---

[45] The United States Strategic Command prepared a "theater Nuclear Planning Document" listing Iraqi targets for a nuclear strike, while Donald Rumsfeld, on the pretext of being reassuring, noted "we will not foreclose the possible use of nuclear weapons if attacked." The reassurance came in the form of a caveat noting, "we can do what needs to be done using conventional capabilities." For a critical discussion, see Nicholas D. Kristof, "Flirting with Disaster," *New York Times*, February 14, 2003, p. A31.

cies, which traditionally make war a last resort to be used only in cases of self-defense or in response to a threat so imminent that it is tantamount to an aggression, must adhere to the very highest standards. To this degree, preventive war and democracy are simply self-contradictory. How can a democracy square the respect it must show for doubt and human frailty and the understanding of unintended consequences it learns from experience with a strategic doctrine that makes no allowances for error in a world where there is no "pluperfect intelligence"?

PART TWO

Lex Humana;

or,

Preventive Democracy

6

Preventive Democracy

> The bond of our common humanity is stronger
> than the divisiveness of our fears and preju-
> dices. God gives us a capacity for choice. We
> can choose to alleviate suffering. We can
> choose to work together for peace."
> —*President Jimmy Carter, 2003*[1]

Nestling in the illicit logic of American exceptionalism, sustained by a belief in the righteousness of Pax Americana and
the efficacy of fear, preventive war doctrine entails not just an
"America First!" notion unsuited to achieving security in an interdependent world but an "Only America!" approach that vests in the
United States prerogatives no other sovereign nation is permitted
to enjoy. An alternative doctrine that addresses terrorism must
allow the United States the right of any sovereign nation to determine the conditions of its own security but must do so in ways con-
sistent with America's own liberal traditions and the imperatives of
international law (which are in fact the same thing).

An effective national security strategy must secure America
against terrorism without destroying the liberty in whose name its

---

[1] Nobel Peace Prize Acceptance Speech, Oslo, Norway, December 10, 2002.

struggle is waged, and it must overcome terror without paying a price in fear. It must propound a strategy that can be a model for any sovereign nation wishing to guarantee its own safety. It must be grounded in realism, not idealism. A high-minded policy that is moral and in accord with law but fails as a prophylactic against terrorist attacks is little better than one that prevents terror but destroys the values in whose name the struggle against it is waged. The strategic doctrine that meets these standards I dub preventive democracy.

Preventive democracy assumes that the sole long-term defense for the United States (as well as other nations around the world) against anarchy, terrorism, and violence is democracy itself: democracy within nations and democracy in the conventions, institutions, and regulations that govern relations among, between and across nations. What democracy means is, of course, contentious, and as I will argue at length below, it means far more that elections and majority rule, and requires a long, painstaking process to be established.

It is a truism that democracies rarely make war on one another. The corollary to that old saw is that democracies rarely produce international terrorism and international violence. Sectarian violence on behalf of ethnic identity or subnational aspirations to independence may nurture violence *within* democracies—as happened with the IRA in Northern Ireland and the ETA in the Basque region of Spain or with "militia" activities within the United States. And radical ideologies like those that animated Germany's Baeder-Meinhof gang or Italy's Red Brigades can trouble the domestic politics of otherwise stable democracies. But the great preponderance of organizations on the State Department's terrorist organization list either operate within undemocratic regimes or are sponsored and supported by undemocratic regimes. They generally operate against democratic regimes, in part because democratic regimes represent supporters of tyranny or occupation, and in part because such open societies are far more hospitable to free and anonymous movement and hence far more vulnerable to terrorist activities than the police states that have often inspired their rage. Where but in America could terrorists bent on destruction find such a welcome and be able to solicit training and logistical support (technical education, flight training, Web programming skills) for their mission, among the very people they aspire to murder?

Despite its erstwhile distaste for "nation building," the Bush administration acknowledges the protection democracy affords against the inroads of terrorism. Thus it aspires now to democratize former enemy regimes like Afghanistan and Iraq and imagines a democracy domino effect, in which democratization sweeps across whole regions like the Middle East. But democracy cannot be imposed at the muzzle of a well-wishing outsider's rifle. It arises not from the ashes of war but from a history of struggle, civic work, and economic development. State-focused preventive war is its least likely parent. Nor is democracy likely to be built from materials exported by a conquering American "liberator" army or in the shadow of American private sector firms and nongovernmental organizations (NGOs). Companies initially invited to bid on the Iraqi reconstruction included Bechtel (and a subsidiary owned in part by the "respectable" side of the bin Laden family), Parson Corporation, and Washington Group International, as well as Kellogg, Brown & Root, a subsidiary of Halliburton (once headed by Vice-President Dick Cheney) that built cells for detainees at Guantá-namo Bay.[2] Democracy grows slowly and requires indigenous

---

[2] Elizabeth Becker, "U.S. Business Will Get Role in Rebuilding Occupied Iraq," *New York Times*, March 18, 2003, p. A18. According to Neil King Jr. of the *Wall Street Journal*: "The Bush administration's audacious plan to rebuild Iraq envisions a sweeping overhaul of Iraqi society within a year of a war's end, but leaves much of the work to private U.S. companies. The Bush plan, as detailed in more than 100 pages of confidential contract documents, would sideline United Nations development agencies and other multilateral organization that have long directed reconstruction efforts in places such as Afghanistan and Kosovo. The plan also would leave big nongovernmental organizations largely in the lurch" ("Bush Has an Audacious Plan to Rebuild Iraq," *Wall Street Journal*, March 17, 2003, p. 1).

struggle, the cultivation of local civic institutions, and a carefully nurtured spirit of citizenship that depends heavily on education. Private sector corporations may secure profits, but the contradictions bred by relying on private capital for public ends was captured by Lawrence Summers in 1995, when he told Congress, "for each dollar the American government contributed to the World Bank, American corporations received $1.35 in procurement contracts."[3] A cynic might suggest today that for each dollar contributed to Republican Party electoral campaigns, friendly corporations can expect a million back in Iraqi reconstruction contracts.[4]

The story of a democratized Germany and a liberalized Japan built from the ashes of World War II's vanquished tyrannies is a touching and exemplary narrative, and it is understandable that advocates of rebuilding postwar nations like Afghanistan and Iraq should appeal to it. But it is a story of failed aggressor nations badly disillusioned by a half century of war facing a post-war world utterly alone, the sea in which their toxic ideologies once floated dried up and vanished; it is a story of cooperation, massive economic support, extensive civic education, long-term American personnel commitments (troops are still in both regions nearly sixty years after the war's end); and it is a story of America's own crucial long-term (and very expensive) commitment to building interna-

---

[3] William Finnegan, "After Seattle," *The New Yorker*, April 17, 2000. Then Clinton official Summers meant this as high praise, not criticism, since he was urging the Congress to support the World Bank.

[4] To take one example, Richard Perle, an adviser to Donald Rumsfeld who formerly served as chairman of the Defense Policy Board, was retained by the now-bankrupt telecommunication company Global Crossing while advising the Pentagon. Six hundred thousand dollars of his $725,000 fee allegedly was contingent on Global Crossing getting Pentagon approval of its sale to a Hong Kong joint venture. See Maureen Dowd, "Perle's Plunder Blunder," *New York Times*, March 23, 2003, sec. 4, p. 13.

tional institutions and creating a system of international law as a framework for economic recovery, civic development, and democratization.[5] This was in fact the framework that made possible both Europe's and Asia's postwar successes. Europe's story is in fact uniquely the story of preventive democracy and may explain the current antipathy there to the American reliance on preventive war. The lip service paid to the Marshall Plan by the Bush administration will only become credible when it can be measured by personnel dedicated to, dollars allocated for, and years expended on making good on the rhetoric. The reality seems to be otherwise. In language striking from strong supporters of the war in Iraq, the editors of the *New Republic* featured a postwar cover story headlined "Mission NOT Accomplished: Bush Prepares to Abandon Iraq."[6]

Preventive democracy as a strategic doctrine entails two equally vital components: First, a military and intelligence component that can be understood as "nonstate-directed preventive war." This limited form of preventive war exclusively targets and destroys terrorist agents, cells, networks, training and armament bases, and organizations. There may be arguments about which groups or individuals qualify as terrorists, but the sovereignty of independent states is not violated in pursuit of them. Second, there is a global democracy-building component—projects like CivWorld (see chapter 9)—that enacts preventive democracy. CivWorld (and many other similar programs) focuses on creating the conditions within and among states that foster the growth of indigenous dem-

---

[5] Unfortunately, it is also a story of Cold War fearfulness and a rapid forgiving and reintegrating of tens of thousands of ex-Nazi middle managers, officers, judges, and administrators into the new "democratic" Germany. See Norbert Frei, *Adenauer's Germany and the Nazi Past: The Politics of Amnesty and Integration* (New York: Columbia University Press, 2003).

[6] Cover, *New Republic*, May 26, 2003.

ocratic institutions and behaviors within nations, as well as global democratic governing institutions and behaviors among them.

Nonstate-directed preventive war pursues the logic of preventive war as it was originally conceived—against stateless martyrs and terrorist individuals and organizations that through their behavior have put themselves at war with the United States and/or its allies. Strictly speaking, preventive war in this setting is defensive rather than preemptive. It is always directed at the declared enemy—terrorists—and never at parties guilty by increasingly remote degrees of association; never, for example, at states that may have helped fund, harbor, sponsor, or have otherwise supported them unless their action constitutes an actual act of war (knowingly supplying a nuclear weapon to a group planning to use it against the United States, for example). Where targeted terrorists are attacked within the sovereign boundaries of an unfriendly state (or even a friendly one, which happened when a terrorist cadre was blown up by an American rocket while it was driving in Yemen), every effort must be made to acknowledge that nation's sovereignty and to treat the intervention as a special case, ideally undertaken with permission (although this will not always be feasible). This tactic effectively exempts the nation whose territorial integrity has been violated from responsibility for the targeted terrorist—the very opposite of what state-focused preventive war currently does. The conceit is that an international terrorist operating within a state is operating outside that state's sovereignty and hence is a fair target.

Such a tactic rests on the illusion, to which both parties must subscribe, that a surgical strike is not an affront to the state's sovereignty; but it is by such illusions that legitimacy and legality are sustained. While it raises its own questions of legitimacy, the tactic is far preferable to preventive war against sovereign states. Call it the "Osirak option," after the hotly debated 1981 one-shot strike by Israel against the Osirak nuclear reactor in Iraq. This was a strike of dubious legitimacy, but because it was limited, directed against a genuine capability to build nuclear weapons of mass destruction, and clearly intended to excise a threat rather than aggress against a nation, the Israelis got away with it.

A relevant American example emerged when the United States learned at the start of 2003 that there was a terrorist cell of the group Ansar al-Islam operating in northern Iraq whose operatives (among them the dangerous Abu Musab al-Zarqawi) had been seen in Baghdad (as well as in Syria, Iran, and other neighboring states). The United States had two options. In keeping with its counter-state preventive war strategy, Secretary Powell used the discovery to buttress his case for preventive war against Iraq in his February 2003 Security Council presentation. But a more appropriate non-state preventive war response would have been to direct a strike on the camp at Khurmal in northern Iraq (not actually a Saddam-controlled region). More than a year earlier, President Bush had spoken derisively about the futility of sending expensive rockets into empty tents in the desert, but the only way to assure an effective war against terrorism is to target the right tents before their occupants have fled. But Ansar al-Islam was the real enemy, and its training camp was the appropriate target, not the various governments in whose territories Ansar operatives traveled, sought medical treatment, made contact, and raised funds (which could easily include countries friendly to or allied with the United States). By the time Khurmal was taken during the Iraqi war, its terrorist inhabitants, if such they were, were long gone.

Preventive war that targets *nonstate* entities can alone justify that novel doctrine's excursion to the edge of legitimacy—and it will normally consist in police and intelligence operations (which have been the most successful elements in President Bush's post-9/11 campaign against terrorism). It represents the near-term military component of a preventive democracy strategy, treating terrorism as an autonomous and mobile parasite living in but not dependent on the body of a host—willing or unwilling. Killing the host leaves the parasite unencumbered, compelling it only to move on to a new host. Either the parasite must be isolated and destroyed (counterterrorist preventive war) or the host body must be made inhospitable to the parasite.

Preventive democracy aims at restoring the health of the infected body and making it less hospitable to parasites. Its most important long-term tactics are civic, economic, cultural, and diplomatic. Such an approach aims over time at a world of democracies interacting in a democratic world. A world of healthy civic democracies would be a world without terror. A world whose international economic, social, and political relations were democratically regulated would be relatively secure from deep inequalities or wrenching poverty and hence less vulnerable to systematic violence.

The animating spirit of a national security strategy based on a preventive democracy doctrine—and the standard by which it must be measured—is above all the national security of the nation, whether it is the United States or any other country. Next comes the security of others. Third come the values and norms that define democracy at its best (whether American or not) and the norms of a lawful and just international system (one hopes these are roughly commensurable). These three sets of objectives should be in harmony, but harmonious or not, the overriding benchmark of any national defense policy must be security—not some metaphor for security or values such as liberty and justice that do not themselves define security. No nation, however idealistic, can be expected to put itself at risk, let alone commit suicide, in the name of its values, however dear. Preventive democracy meets this strict standard. Its virtues are evident when it is measured against thirteen rules that can be distilled from the lessons of history and the exploration of preventive war's logic by which we have arrived at this point in the unfolding argument for preventive democracy. By these same measures, the counterstate preventive war doctrine reveals the flaws that make its consequences for American security so catastrophic.

Thirteen Rules for National Security in the Age of Terror

1. **States are not the enemy;** because terrorists are not states.
2. **War is irrational;** its outcomes cannot be predicted from rules of rational behavior—inaction and action alike have unintended consequences.
3. **War is a last resort**—a "failure" rather than an "instrument of policy."
4. **Going first exacts costs first:** the certain costs of starting a war outweigh the uncertain benefits of "winning" a war because starting costs *must* be paid. Thus, democracies bear a special responsibility to accept the costs of going second.
5. **Terrorism and conventional military power are incommensurable;** so conventional weapons cannot defeat terrorism.
6. **Terrorism's only weapon is fear:** effective national security strategy should diminish rather than augment it, which means fear cannot defeat fear.
7. **Terrorists are international criminals;** when they are captured, they should be treated in conformity with international law.
8. **Weapons of mass destruction mandate "no first strike";** there can be no "tactical" or preemptive use of strategic weapons of mass violence.
9. **Legitimate defense strategies can be universalized;** they must not be grounded in exceptionalism.
10. **Preemption must be applied only to specific targets;** to protect sovereignty, preventive counterterror measures can target only terrorists.

11. Regime change cannot be a rationale for preventive war against terrorism; changing a government from the outside infringes sovereignty without addressing terrorists.

12. A coercive inspections regime is always preferable to war; coercive inspections limit warfare and respect essential sovereignty.

13. Unilateral national security strategies are self-contradictory; unilateralism is a perk of sovereignty but cannot secure safety in an age of interdependence.

Preventive democracy lives up to these rules better than counterstate preventive war on every count. Yet its realization is more daunting than the slogans often associated with it suggest. Indeed, it turns out to be little less difficult to implement effectively than preventive war. It has only two virtues: It steps out of fear's empire, seeking security from terror elsewhere than in countervailing fear. And it works.

7

You Can't Export McWorld and Call It Democracy

If globalization is ruled merely by the laws of the market applied to
suit the powerful, the consequences cannot but be negative.
—*Pope John Paul II*[1]

Global Capitalism does not necessarily bring progress and
prosperity to the periphery. . . . Foreign capital. . . . is also
a potent source of bribery and corruption.
—*George Soros*[2]

The impulse to nurture the growth of democracy is crucial to
preventive democracy understood as a national security policy,
but nurturing democracy is often confounded with the impulse to
export capitalism and cultivate global markets. Many people
believed that in the countries that emerged from the long night of
Soviet communism, dawn was signaled by the rise of free trade and
privatization of capital. In the Clinton no less than the Reagan

[1] Apostolic Exhortation, Mexico City, January 28, 1999; cited in Alessandra
Stanley, "Pope Urges Bishops to Minister to the Rich," *New York Times*, January 24, 1999, sec. 1, p. 10.

[2] Personal correspondence with author, 2000.

administration, the term *market democracy* was used to suggest that democracy is synonymous with the free market, as if a "cold shower" approach to economics involving the abrupt privatization of power and wealth could wash away the sins of the command economy. Communism's totalitarian perversion of the concept of public goods seemed to have made the very idea of the public guilty by association.

Confusing democratization with economic liberalization is to confound the spread of liberty with the spread of McWorld—that seductive compound of American commercialism, American consumerism, and American brands that I have elsewhere argued has dominated the globalization process. When the ethos of Disney becomes synonymous with the ethics of liberty and when consumers come to be seen as identical with citizens, genuine democratization is derailed. Yet this understanding of democratization as marketization goes to the heart of America's postwar nation-building strategy in places like Afghanistan and Iraq. The leading premise is that free markets will breed free women and men, that markets and democracy are pretty much the same thing. Even thoughtful critics of marketization can confuse the building of civic democracy with the spread of markets. In an otherwise persuasive critique of how exporting free markets "breeds ethnic hatred and global instability," Yale Law School professor Amy Chua argues that "the global spread of markets and democracy is a principal, aggravating cause of group hatred and ethnic violence," adding that it is not just the market but democracy itself that is seen as "a panacea."[3] Fareed Zakaria shares a simplistic and unfriendly view of democracy as nothing but elections, but as a friend to markets warns that the real threat comes from democratic theorists who are

[3] Chua, *World on Fire*, pp. 9, 13.

today "mostly radicals in favor of total, unfettered democracy."[4] For Zakaria, unlike Chua, liberal markets do not exacerbate the perils of democracy but ameliorate them. Neoliberalism is not the problem but the solution. "What we need in politics today," he writes— arriving at Chua's conclusion from an opposite direction—"is not more democracy but less."[5]

Given how often American administrations have merged "market" and "democracy" into a single phrase, and given Zakaria's conviction that neoliberal free trade and marketization can alone save democracy from itself, it is not surprising that critics of democracy abroad cannot see the difference between aggressive capitalism and aggressive democracy. But like Amy Chua, such critics risk throwing out freedom's baby while trying to dispose of its economic bathwater. Just how separable market forces and democratization can be is evident from the Bush administration's plans for postwar Iraq. Even before war's onset, the government had invited major private sector American corporations to bid on reconstruction contracts. Critical attention focused on the apparent connections between some members of the administration and the corporations involved (Halliburton, for example), but less attention was paid to the more important fact that reconstruction was being both privatized and Americanized—international NGOs and public institutions being nearly invisible in President Bush's postwar plans, which initially called for a military/civilian administrator (Jay Garner, the head of the Pentagon's new Office of Reconstruction and Humanitarian Assistance, but a former general) under the overall direction of Central Command Commander General Tommy R. Franks but gave way to a civilian, Lewis Palmer Bremer III,

---

[4] Fareed Zakaria, *The Future of Freedom: Illiberal Democracy at Home and Abroad* (New York: W. W. Norton, 2003), p. 245.

[5] Zakaria, *Future of Freedom*, p. 248.

who seemed much more militant. This is civilian control with a difference.

Chua may be right in thinking that markets have swallowed up democracy on the global plane today, but democracy was once capitalism's cage. The historical symmetry that paired democracy and capitalism within societies and made the democratic nation-state the free market's most effective regulator, humanizer, and overseer has gone missing. The marketplace has been globalized willy-nilly, because markets can bleed through porous national boundaries and are not any more constrained by the logic of sovereignty than are SARS, crime, or terrorism. Yet democracy remains trapped inside the nation-state box, leaving global capital utterly unchecked. Today America is not in the business of exporting free market democracy, it is in the business of freeing up markets and globalizing corporate capital and calling it democracy.

The history of capitalism and free markets has long been one of synergy with democratic institutions. But synergy is not identity. Free economies have grown up within and been fostered, constrained, and regulated by democratic states. Democracy has been a precondition for free markets, not the other way round. As representation and suffrage were extended, entrepreneurial capitalism grew up alongside them. Only in the nineteenth century, well after the unwritten British constitution had evolved in clearly democratic directions, did mass industrial capitalism and free trade become hallmarks of the British economy and the British Empire. The freedom of the market that has helped sustain freedom in politics and a spirit of competition in the political domain has itself been historically conditioned by democratic institutions. In the United States, industrial capitalism took off only after the Civil War, when the franchise was extended to universal manhood suffrage. Contract law and regulation as well as civic cooperation and local civic institutions have attenuated capitalism's Darwinist face and contained its tendencies to monopoly, inequality, and other self-destructive contradictions. The gilded age of robber barons ended only when Teddy Roosevelt, Woodrow Wilson, and later Franklin Delano Roosevelt brought the free enterprise system under the regulatory surveillance of the democratic state—not destroying but saving capitalism from its contradictions. In the international sector, the age of robber barons—call them robber banks and outlaw speculators—has returned. For the radically asymmetrical character of globalization has allowed capitalism to leap out of the box defined by nation-state democracy, fostering predatory practices and global anarchy, while leaving democratic institutions behind. It is argued that globalization civilizes and democratizes international relations, but rather it has brutalized them, impelling Pope John Paul II to warn against globalization ruled by the laws of the market and applied to suit the powerful. The neoliberal ideology of privatization that has dominated political thinking in the last several decades and that has been the unspoken context for the American approach to "democratizing" the globe, has in fact had a corrosive effect on democratic governance. In contrast to the religious fundamentalists who fuel terrorism and confront capitalism with destruction, market fundamentalists have made common cause with democracy. Yet market fundamentalism has done little for democracy. It disdains democratic regulation with dogmatic conviction and is as enamored in its own way of global anarchy as the criminal syndicates and terrorist rings it opposes.

The neoliberal orthodoxy believes that markets can do pretty much everything free women and men need done, while government can't do much of anything. From this perspective, democratization's aim ought to be to weaken rather than strengthen state institutions and undermine rather than secure the idea of public goods. Since many societies just emerging from the hold of communist or fundamentalist ideologies have experienced the state only as an exercise in tyranny, this antistate market ideology is not hard to sell. The critique of big government and state bureaucracy quickly becomes a critique of democracy itself. "We the People" morphs into "It the Terrible," and what is supposed to be the march of democracy begins to look like the dismantling not just of the command economy but of popular sovereignty itself. The attack on "big government" turns into an attack on democratic governance.

Privatization ideology softens people up to accommodate the rule of markets. It encourages them to welcome financial capital as a servant of financial capitalists and forget its role as a servant of democratic peoples and their interests. It reverses the traditional logic of social contract thinking on which America was founded and on which an international order must be founded as well. Rather than privilege the power of a common will and public goods over the anarchy of private power, it celebrates private power unencumbered by law, regulation, or government. It insists that freedom is secured not through cultivating justice and the law but by assuring their absence. It denies vehemently the traditional wisdom behind America's historical devotion to multilateralism and international institution building. Thus, it ignores "the secret of the United States' long brilliant run as the world's leading state," described by G. John Ikenberry as "its ability and willingness to exercise power within alliances and multinational frameworks, which made its power and agenda more acceptable to allies and other key states around the world."[6]

Instead, the logic of privatization in the realm of international relations dictates "a general depreciation of international rules,

[6] G. John Ikenberry, "America's Imperial Ambition," *Foreign Affairs,* vol. 81, no. 5 (September/October 2002).

treaties, and security partnerships." Unilateralism is in fact privatization applied to global affairs. Privatizers prefer bilateralism to multilateralism—the best deals involve only two parties. But they prefer unilateralism to either, where there is finally only one party to every contract, the party of power. As Joseph E. Stiglitz wrote of the International Monetary Fund's (IMF's) bilateral practices: "In theory the IMF supports democratic institutions in the nations it assists. In practice, it undermines the democratic process by imposing policies. Officially, of course, the IMF doesn't 'impose' anything. It 'negotiates' the conditions for receiving aid. But all the power in the negotiation is on one side."[7]

Whether or not, as Ikenberry worries, "unchecked U.S. power, shorn of legitimacy and disentangled from the postwar norms and institutions of the international order, will usher in a more hostile international system, making it far harder to achieve American interests," raw power is unlikely to foster democracy. For the insistence that freedom is marked not by the presence of accountable, transparent democratic government but by the absence of all government—of all restraints on markets—effectively equates freedom with anarchy. Since anarchy is also the lawless environment preferred by criminals and terrorists, neoliberals end up as inadvertent partners in crime with their most insidious adversaries. Privatization puts the public sector on the defensive, both within states and in the ethos that governs relations among them.

Privatization does the ideological work of global market eco-

---

[7] Joseph E. Stiglitz, "The Insider: What I Learned at the World Economic Crisis," *New Republic*, April 17, 2000. Stiglitz went on to argue: "Did America and the IMF push policies because we believed the policies would help East Asia or because we believed they would benefit financial interests in the United States and the industrial world? . . . As a participant in these debates, I got to see the evidence. There was none."

nomics inside nation-states, privileging the private interests of corporations and banks and delegitimizing the common goods of the community. National government now becomes an instructed instrument of the private sector rather than participatory assembly of the public sector. In this guise, government is made over into a useful tool of global firms, banks, and markets in such international organizations as the World Trade Organization and the International Monetary Fund—nominally democratic political organizations constituted by sovereign states, but in effect servants of global economic interests that undermine both national sovereignty and democracy. Privatization does not decentralize power; it is not devolution. Rather, it shifts power deployed from the top down that is public, accountable, and transparent to the private sector, where it remains top-down but is now unaccountable and opaque. Privatization effectively gives public power away, yielding it to private elites beyond scrutiny and control. In the name of liberty, it destroys democracy by annihilating the good of the public (the *res publica*) in whose name democratic republics are constituted in the first place.

Under conditions of privatization, citizens do not approach closer to power but are further distanced from it. Something like this happened in Russia after 1989, when power was wrested from the hands of corrupt and (at best) only quasi-legitimate public authorities and put into the hands of private proprietors who were even more corrupt and were wholly illegitimate. To empower private hierarchical bureaucracies in place of inefficient or bungling public bureaucracies may be a victory for instrumental efficiency but it is not a victory for democracy. When President Clinton proclaimed in 1996 that America had reached the "end of the era of big government," he was unfortunately not so much liberating Americans from public bureaucracy and political corruption as introducing them to the new Enron era of private bureaucracy and corporate corruption. In doing so, he inadvertently helped turn the overt market-fundamentalist war on public inefficiency into a covert war on democracy itself.

The consumerist argument contends that marketizing politics actually enhances choice by permitting individuals to participate by voting, not their conscience or their public values but their dollars and euros and yen. The free market supposedly represents a market democracy of individuals who manifest their preferences and express their choices through their spending habits. If choice is the essence of democracy, consumers busy shopping their preferences are surely model citizens. Indeed, by globalizing shopping and consumption, global markets create global citizens where there were none before.

The consumerist understanding of democracy suffers from two fatal errors: it misunderstands what a voluntary choice is, and it misunderstands what the critical difference is between public and private choosing. To be free, voluntary choices must be unconstrained. Without succumbing to the false claims of "false consciousness" (where it is denied that ordinary people know what they are doing when they make consumer choices), one can recognize that how people spend dollars or euros is not always quite as free as it may feel. "Save us from what we want!" reads the postmodern age's best-known secular prayer. The psychology of wants and needs in an era of pervasive consumption surely calls into doubt the term *voluntary*. Freely made choices are subject to marketing, merchandizing, advertising, and packaging influences, all of which (as the billions spent in these sectors suggest) are intended to shape, modify, divert, and even compel choice in the direction of what producers need to sell rather than of what consumers need to buy. In the run-up to the Iraq war, American consumers spent large sums on duct tape, plastic sheeting, bottled water, flashlights, and even gas masks on the recommendation of the Department of Home Security. Did their spending represent "voluntary" consumption or something else?

Traditional capitalism once manufactured goods to meet the felt needs of ordinary people; postmodern capitalism appears more often to manufacture needs to assure the sale of a surfeit of goods for which there may be no need at all among ordinary people. The "need" for duct tape rested entirely on (dubious) government claims that Americans might protect themselves against chemical and biological warfare by sealing up their windows (a position Homeland Security quickly renounced). The need for DVD burners, SUVs, boutique bottled waters, or Hula Hoops is far more problematic. Much of what is for sale in the consumer economy addresses needs created by the producers and little else. Even consumer capitalism's least skeptical celebrants may admit that the billions spent on marketing to children from one to six years old points to something other than pure market freedom and pristine consumer choice.

Even were it to be shown that consumer choosing was always genuinely free and a reflection exclusively or what people "really" want and need, consumer choice remains necessarily a matter of private choice. These private decisions, autonomous or not, cannot affect public outcomes and are not appropriate surrogates for public choices. Democratic governance is not simply about private choice; it is about public choosing: about dealing with the public and social consequences of private choices and behavior.

It is as citizens that consumers and private choosers deal with the public consequences of what they do as private persons. Even classical free market philosophers like Milton Friedman allude to the "neighborhood effects" of private actions that private action itself may not be able to address—environmental pollution, for example.[8] The distinction between private choosing and its social impact is the essence of citizenship, and is intuitively grasped by citizens. Many Americans genuinely want sport utility vehicles, and a number probably believe they need them for reasons (however spurious) of safety, off-road capability, cargo space, and so forth. Yet it is completely rational for an avid SUV fan to want a Humvee as a consumer but as a citizen to make it extremely expensive and/or difficult for anyone (himself as a consumer included) to buy and operate one. As a citizen, a person reckons with the social and public implications of what she does as a consumer. The consumer says, "I feel safer in an SUV." The citizen says, "You may feel that way, but safety data shows you're not, and it certainly proves people in other smaller vehicles are endangered, so we are going to regulate SUVs, make their bumpers conform to uniform standards." The consumer says, "I love that V-8 power surge!" The citizen says, "Yeah, but we need to reduce our dependence on foreign oil, on countries like Iraq and Saudi Arabia, and we need to do more to stop emissions that cause global warming, so we are going to improve gas mileage, treat these suckers as passenger vehicles not light trucks, insist they meet higher emission standards."

This may sound like schizophrenia, but it is simply the difference between consumers and citizens: the consumer within an individual person and the citizen within that person. It is the difference

---

[8] Milton Friedman, *Capitalism and Freedom* (Chicago: University of Chicago Press, 1962), p. 30. Friedman trivializes the idea of public goods or social consequences by using "neighborhood" and goes on to dismiss the argument as a justification for democratic government since. In his too clever words, "when government engages in activities to overcome neighborhood effects, it will in part introduce an additional set of neighborhood effects" summed up in an encroachment on personal liberties (p. 32). A perfectly circular argument.

between "me" thinking and "we" thinking, and hence the difference between private thinking and public thinking, between consumer and civic logic. Democracy's virtue is that it insists on the priority of the we over the me, of civic over consumer logic. The exact balance is the task of democratic politics itself, but no balancing can occur unless the difference between the two is grasped.

The globalization of markets and of the consumer mentality has meant that global reasoning is dominated by private consumerist logic rather than public civic logic. In addressing mobile financial capital, for example, the relevant question according to consumer logic becomes how to protect the investor rather than how to protect the public goods his investment feigns to enhance but in practice often damages. A market-biased system of the kind that defines globalization today will sacrifice the common welfare needs of an entire people in the name of forcing governments to promote budgetary "discipline" so that speculative capital is secured. Rather than relying on high returns to repay those who engage in high-risk investment, investors insist on high returns but low risks that are in effect secured by forcing governments to take the real risks. Modern global capitalism thereby manages to privatize profit while socializing risk.

Neoliberal ideology argues that regulations that protect common needs encroach unfairly on the liberty necessary to the free flow of capital, labor, and goods. Much the same thing was said about the introduction of unions in the late nineteenth century, when organizing labor around its common interests was seen as an infringement both of the liberty of producers to hire workers at free market wages and of the "right to work" of laborers free to accept a given wage or refuse the job.

The marketplace, local and global, offers a perfect venue for the expression of economic preferences and for the arbitration of relations between producers and consumers. But even when its workings are not skewed by unevenly distributed power and the pressures of monopoly, even when merchandizing and marketing do not pervert the meaning of needs and wants, the market cannot secure public goods or outcomes conducive to the general welfare. Free market fundamentalists claimed the public interest would be forged from a magical intersection of private wills—manipulated by what Adam Smith called the "invisible hand"—but this was never more than a dream, an unconvincing rationalization for privileging those who actually benefited from private market exchanges.

Democracy is the mechanism by which private power and personal desires are accommodated to public goods and the common weal. Aggregating private interests will not do this job because power too gets aggregated, along with interests, resulting in skewed and unfair outcomes. But market theory is oblivious to power. It assumes equality and relatively perfect competition. Yet power is the essence of human relations and stalks every "voluntary" choice and every "freely made" contract. The public good is not simply the sum of private goods but the equalization of power according to rules of fairness and justice, something markets simply cannot achieve.

The most dangerous forms of tyranny are those that are advanced under the banner of freedom. Hence Pope John Paul II's trenchant warning that "the human race is facing forms of slavery which are new and more subtle than those of the past, and for too many people, freedom remains a word without meaning."[9] To take but one egregious example, when freedom is associated with the privatization of goods as obviously public as the human genome, the pope's fears are vindicated. Freedom must mean something more than corporate profit and consumer choice.

[9] Pope John Paul II, "Incarnationis Mysterium," Bull of Indiction of the Great Jubilee of the Year 2000, Rome, November 29, 1998.

In Federalist Number 63, the prescient James Madison wrote that "liberty may be endangered by the abuses of liberty, as well as by the abuses of power . . . and the former rather than the latter is apparently most to be apprehended by the United States." Nowhere today are the abuses of liberty more evident than in the made-in-America global market sector, where in the good name of liberty monopoly, greed, narcissism, and anarchy have been set loose; and where global private capital, consumer narcissism, and rampant commercialism pass as harbingers of global democracy.

Owls hope that what happens after wars of "liberation" is as important as what happens during them. The Bush administration is publicly committed to democratization. But to think that exporting McWorld and globalizing markets is tantamount to forging free societies and a democratic world is a dangerous misconception likely to undermine prospective nation-building strategies. To democratize nations emerging from despotism and to endow an anarchic global disorder with an infrastructure of public law and civic cooperation cannot be simply to export capitalism. *Luxus Americana* cannot be confounded with lex humana. Preventive democracy must look elsewhere for recipes that will end terrorism and promote both safety and freedom.

8

You Can't Export America and Call It Freedom

Ultimately the best strategy to ensure our security and to build a
durable peace is to support the advance of democracy elsewhere.
—*President Bill Clinton, 1994*[1]

Better to let them do it imperfectly than to do it perfectly yourself,
for it is their country, their way, and your time is short.
—*T. E. Lawrence*[2]

xporting markets or globalizing neoliberal ideology evidently
will not democratize other nations or forge a democratic
global sector. But nor can democracy itself be treated as a viable
product for export. The goal of preventive democracy is a democratized world but this does not mean exporting American democracy. It is heartening that despite its penchant for war and its
prejudices against "Clinton-style" nation building, the Bush administration has come to understand that destabilized and defeated
states, even if cleansed of terrorists and WMD, offer little long-
term security for the Unites States and its allies. Yet it has not yet
grasped that attempting to nation-build by force, trying to make

---

[1] State of the Union Address, January 25, 1994.

[2] Quoted in George Packer, "Dreaming of Democracy," *New York Times Magazine*, March 2, 2003.

other nations free by exporting American democracy to their shores, is unlikely to succeed.

On behalf of stability and democracy, the administration promised to do in Iraq what it promised to do in Afghanistan, as earlier administrations had promised to do in Kuwait, though what has happened in those countries does not hold out much promise for success. "Kuwaitis have waited 12 years for promised reforms that never came," and according to the *Washington Post*, although parliamentary elections were held in 1992, 1996, and 1999 for the 14 percent of Kuwait's 860,000 citizens eligible to vote (the rest are women, foreign residents, and guest workers) the "balloting has produced a parliament in which the strongest political forces are conservative tribal leaders allied with Islamic fundamentalists, some of whom proclaim sympathy for Palestinian suicide bombers and Osama bin Laden."[3] It is too soon to judge outcomes in Afghanistan, but although the United States authorized $3.3 billion in new U.S. aid to Afghanistan over four years (about $850 million per annum), legislation passed by the Congress in 2002–2003 called for only $157–$295 million for the current year (an item at first left out of the budget entirely). Nor has the United States wanted to use the United Nations as a legitimizing instrument or to engage international nongovernmental organizations or allied governments as nation-building partners in Iraq, opting to depend on private American companies and charitable organizations with shared ideological perspectives such as Frank Graham's Christian Charity. In Afghanistan, groups like Children of War, Islamic Relief Fund, CARE, Save the Children, and Terre des Hommes, as well as United Nations organizations such as the UN Center for Human

---

[3] Susan B. Glasser, "A Model for Democracy?," *Washington Post National Weekly Edition*, March 3–9, 2003. Kuwait is developing its civil society, but "it is a place without a single legally recognized human rights organization."

Settlements and UNESCO, eventually all played a role in reconstruction. President Karzai's older brother founded Afghans for Civil Society, a cross between a policy center and a humanitarian organization, which has labored to ground the country's uncertain experiment in democratization in a civil foundation. But in Iraq, America's go-it-alone posture has dominated early postwar reconstruction efforts. The impolitic insistence on punishing both the United Nations and allies such as France, Germany, and Turkey who refused to support the war effort has made it nearly impossible to involve them or NGOs associated with them in the work of democratization.

Democratization can be further impeded by the circumstances that lead to so-called liberation. It should be clear to anyone who reads history that democracy cannot be imposed on a country at the point of a gun or in the troubled wake of a war of aggression, even a "preventive" one launched in the name of benevolent regime change and freedom. George Packer notes that of eighteen "forced" regime changes in which the United States played a role in the last century, only five resulted in democracy—make that one (Panama) when America intervened uniltaterally.[4] Nor is the triumphant nation by whom a tyrant has just been vanquished necessarily the ideal overseer of an indigenous democratization process, which is probably why T. E. Lawrence preferred autonomous insufficiency to imposed perfection. The lex humana in whose name internationalism and global democracy must be pursued will not be secured by trying to export lex Americana—America's own unique experience with law and democracy.[5]

[4] Packer, "Dreaming of Democracy."

[5] As Howard J. Wirda argues, American notions of civil society are also difficult to export, and often are greeted with distrust by governments who fear an erosion of their power. See "Is Civil Society Exportable? The American Model and Third World Development," working paper, Nonprofit Sector Research Fund, Aspen Institute, 2003.

Democracy can't be exported because rights can't be imported. The Belgium civil rights activist Dyab Abou Jahjah may frighten Europeans with his angry rhetoric, but the manifesto of his Arab European League gets one thing right: "You do not receive equal rights," it proclaims, "you take them."[6] That was also the cry of Americans in 1776, when they declared their intention to secure their rights and their democracy in an armed struggle against England. France inaugurated its uneven march to democracy with a brutal and violent revolution against an absolute monarchy. Postcolonial nation building in Africa and Asia after World War II originated in armed struggle and was not bequeathed by the colonizing imperial powers being contested, even when they were democracies. Democracy cannot be gifted to an unwilling people or imported into a culture not ready for it. It depends on the passion of people who strive for liberty rather than the beneficence of benign masters prepared to grant them liberty. Echoing the Bush administration, Prime Minister Blair spoke about Iraq as Nazi Germany, and America and Britain as the Allies during World War II, warning them against appeasing a rogue regime capable of inflicting grievous damage on the world. But at least some Iraqis along with many of their Middle Eastern neighbors—who otherwise held no brief for Saddam Hussein—appeared to believe Iraq was more like Poland facing a powerful enemy invading sovereign territory on the pretext of self-defense: not an ideal start for the democratization process.

Democracy's most important virtue is, in fact, patience. Indeed, it is a necessary condition for its development. In France, for example, Tocqueville portrayed the revolution of 1789 as completing rather than inaugurating processes of centralization and rational

---

[6] Marlise Simons, "An Outspoken Arab in Europe: Demon or Hero?," *New York Times*, March 1, 2003, p. A4.

bureaucratization that were prequels to real democratization. The slow movement toward modernity had begun much earlier with the abolition of the feudal provincial *parlements* and the assertion of the king's modern rights over those of the feudal aristocracy.[7] In the United States, 150 years of slow cultivation of local democratic institutions in the thirteen colonies preceded the making of what was in any case only a quasi-democratic constitution.[8] Another century and a quarter passed before something resembling full democracy was secured, and this protracted period was marked by robust democracy only for a minority, white males who were citizens. Otherwise, the American story reflected an ongoing exclusion of the majority of the population from citizenship. A slave system coexisted with the burgeoning local democracy celebrated by Tocqueville and was terminated only by a devastating civil war.

Yet Americans today sometimes seem to think other people in cultures new to democracy should achieve in a few months what it took Americans and other mature democracies centuries to secure. No time for mistakes, no time to build a civic foundation on which to ground a democratic superstructure, no time to educate women and men for citizenship, no time to cultivate the arduous habits of the heart essential to democratic behaviors. In the media-driven quarterly profit sheet–style timetables that today define the American nation-building agenda for others, there is never time. How

---

[7] See Alexis de Tocqueville, *The Ancien Regime and the French Revolution* (1856). Tocqueville himself actually associated the *parlement* with ancient liberty and their destruction with a loss of liberty, but in this he was a critic of modern centralized egalitarianism. Simon Schama takes up this theme in his conservative portrait of the revolution in *Citizens: A Chronicle of the French Revolution* (New York: Alfred A. Knopf, 1989).

[8] Oscar and Lilian Handlin's *Liberty and Power: 1600–1760* (New York: Harper & Row, 1986) offers a vivid picture of this slow and deliberate nurturing of democratic institutions in prerevolutionary colonial America.

could policymakers in the White House have really believed that Iraq's violent, unstable, multicultural society held together by brute tyranny for thirty years could be both liberated and liberalized overnight? Iraq is dominated demographically by disempowered Shiites who outnumber Saddam Hussein's ruling Sunnis; it is tribal, even clannish, in its sectarian loyalties; it is encumbered by Kurdish and other minority populations in the north and the south whose only real "nation-building" ambition is partition and autonomy; it is threatened by Turks from the north and Iranian Shiites from the east with their own agendas of expansion. Is such a nation to be jerked around into a model Middle Eastern democracy in a few months? Or years? Or decades? Ongoing instability, looting, and criminality (asylums and prisons were emptied), tribal infighting, and civil war of the kind that afflicted Yugoslavia following the defeat of communism there are more likely in Iraq than instant democracy. Such national breakdown has already prompted the deferring of an interim government and may mandate prolonged U.S. military rule—hardly a prescription for self-government.[9]

This is not to imply, as some commentators do (Samuel Huntington and Bernard Lewis, for example), that democracy and Islam or democracy and non-Western culture stand in a tension to one another so radical that democratization is highly improbable if not altogether impossible (see below). Challenging the claim that Asia is bound by narrowly authoritarian values, economist Amartya Sen has written wisely about the variety that can be found in every culture and about the ways in which supposedly Western notions such

[9] At the time of the war's onset there were significant differences in the Bush administration about the role of the military in a postwar Iraq, with the Pentagon far less amenable to extended military governance than the State Department. See, for example, Lawrence F. Kaplan, "Federal Reserve: The State Department's Anti-democracy Plan for Iraq," *New Republic*, March 17, 2003.

as tolerance and freedom can be found in Buddhist or Confucian traditions. In his words, "the fact is that in any culture, people seem to like to argue with one another, and frequently do exactly that—given the chance. The presence of dissidents makes it problematic to take an unambiguous view of the 'true nature' of local values. In fact, dissidents tend to exist in every society."[10] Muslim societies left behind by long-term despotic governance and not yet fully equipped culturally to support modern political institutions can probably achieve fully democratic societies within a generation or two, much more rapidly than England, France, and America democratized and domesticated their own once zealous Christian monocultures, and they will. But not on America's timetable. Not tomorrow or next summer.

Forgetting their own gradualist democratic history, Americans too often not only urge others to do it quick and do it easy. They also urge others to do it à l'Americain, as if Americanization and democratization are the same thing, as if the United States has proprietary rights in and a political patent on the quintessential democratic process. There are, to be sure, universal ideals that undergird the human struggle for freedom everywhere, but democracy's forms are as various as the struggles through which it is won and as distinctive as the myriad cultures that win it. They are as difficult to secure as all noble human aspirations are difficult to secure. In the years before the American Revolution and between the Declaration of Independence and the Constitution, Puritan Massachusetts had one constitution, progressive Pennsylvania another, free Rhode Island still another, and the royal charter colonies of the slave plantation South still others. Some colonies were much less free than others, and a few were hardly less autocratic than the background

---

[10] Amartya Sen, *Development as Freedom* (New York: Alfred A. Knopf, 1999), p. 247.

colonial government of Great Britain under which they all labored. America's regional and local institutions are marked by differences that can be traced to such variations even today.

The argument of preventive democracy is that the war against terrorism can succeed only in a world of peaceful democracies, that war and the annihilation of sovereignty are less than ideal instruments for converting tyrannical regimes into democratic ones. Nor are soldiers ideal guides for mapping the topography of democratization in cases where wars do precede democratic development. Representatives of the conquerors will be inappropriate advisers to the conquered on the thorny issues of how to reestablish autonomy, restore domestic credibility, and achieve global legitimacy—especially where society is simultaneously being radically transformed at other levels as well. That was the wisdom of Richard Cheney when he asked how an American-backed regime in a 1991 postwar Iraq could possibly look legitimate. Such wisdom today argues for United Nations support for preventive wars so that United Nations support and involvement in peace afterward is guaranteed. Ridding a state of terrorists, even a state reluctant to be "cleansed," can remove at least one obstacle from the process of democracy building and is a justification for counterterrorist preventive strikes. But ridding a state of its sovereign regime, however unsavory and brutal that regime may be, is likely to put obstacles in the way of rather than facilitate democracy building later—a lesson the U.S. government learned the hard way in the increasingly chaotic weeks following its easy military victory in Iraq.

Democracies grow from inside out and from bottom up rather than from outside in and top down. This is one of the reasons why democratization takes so long. It also suggests that the objective for those seeking a democratic world ought not to be "democracy" in the singular, on the American model or any other, but "democracies" in the plural. After all, even within the parochial Western democratic canon, democratic practices have been as variable as the distinctive European and North American cultures in which they originated. Switzerland, for example, has nurtured a communal and collectivist notion of freedom and public rights at considerable odds with the Anglo-American focus on individuals and private rights. There, the freedom of the commune has always trumped private property rights. In part the consequence of a dairy economy, where common grazing rights trump the proprietary rights typical of agricultural economies, the emphasis on communal freedom has stamped Swiss political institutions with a communitarian character at radical variance with radically individualist American institutions.[11] The Swiss prefer collective to individual leadership (the presidency rotates among the seven members of the Federal Council) and make the citizenry the legislature of first resort (citizens vote on referenda nationally and locally up to several dozen times a year). The representative system on which American politics is so firmly based has far less resonance in Switzerland's direct democracy.

Or compare the French judicial system, rooted in a Cartesian view of Truth—something to be discovered by a panel of objective, investigative judges and developed inside a system of written (Roman) law—with the Anglo-American common law tradition, where judicial truth is subjective and contested, something to be hammered out through a process of adversarial argumentation by prosecutors and defenders arguing pro and con. In this common law tradition, it is the people (via the jury system) rather than expert judges who have the final say. Neither the French system of justice nor the Swiss system of communal and participatory democracy are more or less democratic than their American counterparts.

[11] In an early book, I tried to take the measure of these startling differences: see *The Death of Communal Liberty: The History of Freedom in a Swiss Mountain Canton* (Princeton: Princeton University Press, 1974).

Liberty is vouchsafed in each, even if it is variously interpreted from one to another. The sovereignty of the people is the starting point for legitimacy in all three systems, but whether that sovereignty is directly expressed or represented by elected officials or by reflective judges is differently understood. Justice is the object of law in any democracy, but there may be contrary views of how it is secured in different democratic systems of jurisprudence. In short, there is no Western democracy, there are only Western democracies.

Surely the plurality of Western democracy argues for an appreciation of variety in considering democratization in transitional societies beyond Europe and North America. As Amartya Sen has insisted, it is critically important to recognize "diversity within different cultures" as well as diversity among cultures.[12] In nations and cultures emerging from nondemocratic regimes, it may be more productive in establishing liberty to draw on indigenous traditions and institutions than to mimic exogenous constitutions and important alien political devices.

The American founders insisted from the very outset that the American republic was to be an "experiment," as every democratic founding in fact is. The Federalist Papers were at pains to show why Europe's traditional political theory and long experience with constitutions were of little relevance in the new world. According to *The Federalist*, Europe's democracies had "ever been spectacles of turbulence and contention." Madison had no desire to see America join that "infinity of little, jealous, clashing, tumultuous commonwealths, the wretched nurseries of unceasing discord" that had marked Europe's early history.[13] Instead it would look to its

[12] Sen, *Development as Freedom*, p. 247. Sen notes, for example, that "the reading of Confucianism that is now standard among authoritarian champions of Asian values does less than justice to the variety within Confucius's own teachings" (p. 234).

[13] The first quote is from Federalist Number 10, the second from Federalist Number 9.

own independent colonial experience, its township meetings, its civic militias, its experiments with representation, federalism, and the separation of powers, and it would dare to forge a novel constitution suited to America's novel circumstances. This was one of the healthier lessons of American exceptionalism, but one which Americans have too often failed to apply to other nations. Having abjured the obvious British sources of its founding constitution, the United States ought not to find it so hard to see why others today might abjure the obvious American sources of their own aspirations to independence and democracy. Even where they admire and borrow from America, as prudent new democracies should and will, they need also to search for innovative democratic practices in appropriate local sources and historical traditions that will endow their liberty with a sense of propriety and ownership. FedExing a copy of the Bill of Rights to Kabul or emailing Baghdad a blueprint for a bicameral legislature will probably not do the job.

Historical practices conceived in predemocratic times may yield protodemocratic behaviors that can be incorporated into modern democratic practices. Tribal councils in Africa offer a model of participation and community on which more inclusive participatory institutions can be built. The national tribal convocation (the Loya Jirga), which has from time to time been used to soothe strained relations among warring rivals in tribal Afghanistan, has shown some potential in ameliorating sectional rivalries that imperil national unity there today. Some of the failures of democracy in Africa can be traced to the way in which traditional tribal boundaries were displaced by artificial colonial frontiers, and allowing such boundaries to be reflected in local administrative departments can help tribalism adjust to democracy's demands. The Indian village community is a natural vessel for local participation that, as Gandhi understood, might be preferable in bolstering Indian democracy to the kinds of contrived administrative units bequeathed by the British Empire. The Russian workers council (soviet), before it was deformed into an instrument of one-party Bolshevik rule, acted as a protodemocratic institution in faltering czarist Russia.

Sometimes even the revival of traditional monarchy in a constitutionally delimited form can help a nation's transition from a brutal modern tyranny into liberal democracy by providing a solidarity and patriotism (represented by the monarch) otherwise absent in the formal legal institutions of a newly minted democracy. Kingship, even when embedded in a constitutional order, may seem an odd ally of democracy, but none of the traditional institutions noted here are fully democratic and the restoration of a constitutional monarchy in a nation more recently reduced to abject tyranny can play a useful role in restoring civic legitimacy. Local institutions have democratic potential and have the great additional virtue of rooting the novelty of formal democracy in traditional informal practices already legitimatized by a nation's history and usage. Local urban political clubs in nineteenth-century America, although they looked to some critics a little too much like gangs, nevertheless provided a first entry into political participation for immigrants and outsiders—at the price, to be sure, of both hierarchy and corruption. So, too, indigenous institutions elsewhere in the world, even where they exact a price in the purity of their democratic spirit, may offer important stepping stones in the slow process of securing real democratic behaviors and practices in a transitional culture. The fast track to democracy often derails nations in a hurry to be free. A slower, more deliberate pace allows history's curves to be negotiated and assures that the grafting of new institutions on ancient practices has ample time to take. Rooting democracy takes time: sowing its seeds on hard and barren soil assures they will be blown away in the first political gale.

Democracy is, after all, a process not an end, and it moves in stages. The patience of process needs to be recognized as indispensable to the success of those who today have embarked on the difficult journey. Impatience arising out of some democratic overseer's timetable is disastrous, particularly when its benchmarks are borrowed from the stories of other quite different "successful" democracies. Monitoring corruption as the NGO Amnesty International has done is of real importance as long as it is understood that some corruption may be unavoidable in opening up a closed society. Linking development assistance and loans to progress in building legal and civic infrastructure, as the World Bank and the American State Department are doing, makes good sense if it is appreciated that funding must actually find its way to the groups and institutions who build that infrastructure. The goal must be movement in a democratic direction, stages in the growth of liberty that are progressive and not regressive, but not movement that is impressively rapid yet superficial and fragile because monitors and funders refuse to grant others the time lines their own democratization once demanded.

The sad, short history of indigenous democratic practices in East Germany, practices that were crucial in fomenting the 1989 collapse of communism there, is testimony to the costs of impatience—of trying to produce democracy on the quick. The local forums and neighborhood minimedia broadsides and public gatherings under the aegis of *Neues Forum* that prompted successful resistance to the Soviet-dominated East German regime were quickly displaced after the fall of the Wall by West German federal political institutions, national parties, and media conglomerates. Almost overnight, the magic surrounding democratization was dispelled, replaced by an impatience and hubris that drove a wedge between the newly united peoples of East and West Germany. The energy with which the physical Wall had been dismantled yielded all too rapidly to a crippling lassitude associated with what Germans referred to as *der Mauer im Kopf.* This "wall inside the heads" of Germany's two rival nations psychically separated East and West as profoundly as the real Wall had once separated them physically. It also transformed the former subjects of Communist East Germany, the expectant potential citizens of a new united Germany, into cynical and despairing political spectators to a "democratic politics" they could not claim as their own. No wonder so many reverted within a few years to voting for whatever far-left party had succeeded the discredited Communists or whatever far-right party was ready to pick up the antidemocratic slack.

The same tin ear for variety evident in West Germany's inability to acknowledge the East's uniqueness, apart from its communist past, can be detected in the ardent advocates of Samuel Huntington's "clash of civilizations" thesis postulating that there is no room in Islamic society's "antimodern" culture for democracy.[14] But what critics like Huntington actually seem to mean is that there is no room in Islamic societies for *American* democracy: for the separation of church and state as it is inflected in America with its insistent secularism, its laissez-faire approach to morals and religion that trivializes them as essentially private matters, and its relativist presumption that religion is wholly subjective and personal. These are certainly biases of the current American viewpoint. But America in the nineteenth century and, more recently, Catholic democracies in Italy and Latin America have accommodated themselves quite well to a more public theology without abjuring their democratic constitutions.

In fact, it has been a tenet of modern political theory that democracies lacking values anchored in ethics and religious con-

---

[14] See Samuel P. Huntington, *The Clash of Civilizations and the Remaking of World Order* (New York: Simon & Schuster, 1996), and my "Fantasy of Fear: Huntington and the West versus the Rest," *Harvard International Review*, vol. 20, no. 1 (Winter 1997–98). A weaker form of the same claim can be found in the writing of Bernard Lewis.

viction risk both their solidarity and unity and their democratic via-
bility. As a democracy is pulled willingly apart by its commitment
to political liberty and civic pluralism, it must be able to unite
around common religious belief (as Tocqueville observes in
Democracy in America). Because they tend to be fractured and
fractious, pluralistic and open, free societies in search of a common
civic spirit often resort to common civic beliefs that constitute a
kind of civil religion. America's civic faith is embodied in a civil cat-
echism that includes (among others) such documents as the Declaration of Independence, the Constitution and Bill of Rights,
Elizabeth Cady Stanton's Seneca Falls Declaration, the Emancipa-
tion Proclamation, Lincoln's Gettysburg Address, and Martin
Luther King Jr.'s "I Have a Dream" speech. However, it is more
often America's aggressive market materialism and intolerant secularism that is experienced by religious societies confronting Americans hoping to "save" them from theocracy. Why would this not
feel as threatening to Muslim (or, for that matter, Jewish or Christian) peoples as aggressive theocracy feels to the secular liberal
societies of the West? Protestant fundamentalists inside the United
States are as anxiety ridden by the secular culture of consumption
as some of their Muslim brothers in Tehran or Cairo. Otherwise
quite secular parents raised in the bustling shops of the mall still
worry that their children may read too little, shop too much, and
make television rather than schools their primary tutors in acquiring the crucial values that will guide their lives.

Viewed dispassionately, it seems clear that there is no easy way,
certainly no single way, to integrate religion and democratic institutions. Nor are the tensions between Islam and the West or
between Muslim culture and the open society especially unique.
Similar frictions can be detected in the struggle of Christianity,
Judaism, Buddhism, or Hinduism to accommodate their theologies
to the demands of free secular governance. Hindu fundamentalism

today, as manifested in the zealous ideology of the ruling Baratiya Janata Party (BJP), offers challenges to Indian democracy as formidable as any faced by Islamic nations. Although Christianity adopted a "two swords" policy long ago under medieval Pope Gregory that supposedly ceded distinct powers and jurisdictions to the ecclesiastic and secular realms (to pope and emperor), not even America's wall of separation between church and state has managed to fully disentangle them. Yet Christianity's checkered history of conflict with secular governance and democracy teaches important lessons about how a once intolerant and overweening theology can come not only to accommodate but to undergird the growth of democratic institutions.

The necessary tensions associated with religion and politics grow out of the friction between the many human domains that define human plurality—between the profane and the sacred, the private and the public, the worldly and the transcendental. At one pole is the danger of theocracy—the triumph of religion over politics and the consequential annihilation of the boundaries that otherwise separate the realms of life in a healthy culture. But at the other pole is the danger of radical secularism—the triumph of secular markets and aggressive materialism over manners, mores, and religion. This is but another form of the annihilation of boundaries.

Islam no more prohibits the development of democracy than secularism assures it. Varying degrees of democracy have been established in such Muslim states as Bangladesh, Turkey, Bahrain, Tatarstan, Indonesia, Morocco, and Tunisia, and even in Pakistan Shiite mullahs are taking a pro-democracy line. Seraj ul-Haq, a provincial cabinet minister with Pakistan's largest religious party (Jamaat-e-Islami), insisted recently, for example, "We are still Islamists, but we are also democrats. . . . In our campaign, we promised to bring sharia [Islamic law] to the people, but that means building a welfare state, not chopping off hands."[15] The roads to democracy are many, and its cartography belongs to no one nation. A respect for differentiation and variety is as important as patience in cultivating its many forms. Religion secures the solidarity and community of a free society and offers it a firm foundation for its moral and political obligations. According to the Declaration of Independence, it is after all the "Creator" who endows men with the "unalienable Rights" to "Life, Liberty and the Pursuit of Happiness" on which America's civic faith is founded; it is "Nature's God" whose authority puts these rights above government and the courts. Their sacred trust is above all to render them inviolable. Thus does the democratic state call on religion to secure the foundations of its belief in freedom and rights, even as it holds the institutional church at arm's length.

Yet if religion generally places no permanent obstacles in the way of democracy, fundamentalist religion, above all in its Islamist manifestations, would seem to present special problems. This has become clear in the aftermath of the war in Iraq, where democratization has run square up against Shiite Islam. The issue is sharpened when a nation undergoing democratization is emerging not only from tyranny but from tyranny with a secularist edge, such as with Nasser's nationalists in Egypt in the 1950s, the shah's modernizing regime in Iran in the 1960s and '70s, or with the Baathists in Iraq (and in Syria, where they still rule). Where tyranny has been theocratic (as under the Taliban and under the ayatollahs of Iran recently), democratization may be associated with secularization,

---

[15] Cited by Pamela Constable, "Pakistan's Mullah's Speak Softly," *Washington Post*, March 22, 2003, p. A12. For a view of Tatarstan's transition from Soviet totalitarianism to Islamic authoritarian democracy under the watchful eye of Russia, see Bill Keller, "Learning from Russia: Here's a Model for How to Shape a Muslim State," *New York Times*, May 4, 2003, sec. 4, p. 1.

FEAR'S EMPIRE

but where tyranny wears a secular mask, the war on tyranny and the war on secularism may appear as identical.

Under these circumstances, when America's aggressive materialism allies itself with secular authoritarians (Egypt or Pakistan, for example), it is easy for opposition to authoritarianism to mutate into opposition to secularism, and then—when the United States supports democracy—into opposition to democracy. Moreover, given that fundamentalism turns religion's natural tension with the secular state into implacable opposition, Islamism would appear to create special problems. Most religions, however, retain a fundamentalist streak even after they have become more worldly. Government is focused on the living, temporal body and its worldly needs, while religion has a transcendental dimension that looks towards the soul and its otherworldly origins and destiny. Islam is hardly alone in this. In its early "purist" phase, Christianity's otherworldliness obdurately refused to submit to temporal authority at all and was appropriately seen as endangering the very legitimacy of secular rule. There are fundamentalist Jews today who doubt the very legitimacy of the Jewish state of Israel. Fundamentalist Hindus, I have already noted, control India today, while American Protestant fundamentalists such as Franklin Graham (Billy Graham's son) not only dub Islam "a very evil and wicked religion" but assail America's sexed and soulless secular society with the ardor of the ayatollahs they detest.[16] Far greater numbers of Christian Americans (not all of them fundamentalists) invoke religious values

---

[16] Despite Graham's harsh comments on Islam (on *NBC Nightly News* in November 2001), his organization, Samaritan's Purse, has been invited into postwar Iraq as a charitable organization. See Michelle Cottle, "Bible Brigade," *New Republic*, April 21, 2003. Other American fundamentalists suggested that 9/11 was God's punishment on a godless nation, underscoring the strange schizophrenia with which America is perceived in the world, as a harbinger of materialist secularism but stalked internally by fanatic religious fundamentalists as antimodern as the Islamicists America so fears.

to underwrite their political views on abortion or embryonic cell research.

Indeed, within Western secular democracy, fundamentalists often see themselves as a beleaguered minority for which the supposedly liberal secular society shows little real tolerance. Believers elsewhere in the world, besieged by a globalizing commercial culture associated with both America and with democracy, see democratization as a species of covert secularization, a Trojan Horse in which an army of consumer-contaminated merchandisers is concealed. They have a point. Where once it was religion that dominated culture and society and where once it was those alternative (minority) believers in others religions (or no religion at all) who felt in need of protection from the dominant paradigm, today in the era of global commerce and McWorld's cultural homogeneity, it is increasingly the believers who feel imperiled. Adrift in a sea of secularism where their ardent religious convictions are portrayed as aberrant or reactionary, they cannot but regard modernity and Westernization, and thus sometimes democratization, as forerunners of secularization and the destruction of their cultures.

Critics of fundamentalism will protest that Islamism is a proselytizing and intolerant doxology intolerant of "infidels." But fundamentalism is itself a product of culture under siege, and its vulnerable adherents believe they are besieged by a proselytizing and intolerant materialist culture that leaves little real room for the "religious variety" in whose name liberalism preaches its own liberal doxology. The West speaks the grammar of pluralism, but the idiomatic reality sounds to others more like Hollywood homogeneity and is understandably feared as the force behind democratization—above all when democratization is equated with marketization.

Religion, even fundamentalist religion, is capable of reconciling itself with democracy then. But pluralism, an aspect of democracy, does confront fundamentalist believers with serious issues and these cannot be glossed over. Majoritarianism is not a problem for fundamentalists: a religious majority, whether it is comprised of Protestants in nineteenth-century America, Catholics in twentieth-century Ireland, or Hindus in twenty-first-century India, has a perfect right to govern. Majority rule is a key part (though hardly all) of what democracy means. If the 60 percent of Iraqis who are Shiites organize politically and win democratic elections, Shia rule will both embody democracy and imperil liberty. It is liberal pluralism not democracy that stands in special tension with religious rule, but this is only a restatement in a religious context of the generic problem democracy faces in reconciling majority rule with minority rights—the problem of majoritarian tyranny. Democracy is about self-government and majority rule, as well as about liberty, governmental limits, and minority rights. The first is achieved through political participation and elections, the second through limits on power and boundaries between society's plural sectors. If religion—even theocracy—challenges democracy, it is because majoritarianism is not the whole of democracy and democracy is not the whole of popular sovereignty under the constitutional rule of law. But again, this suggests that democratization in Islamic societies raises issues common to all democracies—and certainly all democracies in societies where religion is culturally important—rather than issues unique to Islam.

Paul Berman's claim (in his *Terror and Liberalism*) that radical Islam is a form of totalitarianism is a dangerous distortion that singles out Islamic fundamentalism for problems endemic to all religion and treats religious majoritarianism as distinct from majoritarianism *tout court*. Like other religions, Islam is chary of the boundaries that try to wall off morality from politics and individual salvation from common laws. Shia or the Muslim codes of dress and behavior that elicit the outrage of secular Westerners are in fact only instances of sumptuary laws that exist in nearly every society in human history and that are plenty familiar in Western democracies ("blue laws" in Massachusetts for example, or tavern "closing hours" in England and Germany). They stand in some tension with secularism but are neither undemocratic nor even necessarily illiberal. Many secular rationalists regard Sunday shop closings as a secular blessing that protects one day a week from rampant commercialism. As always, the question is one of degree, something that is negotiated in every culture, especially as societies grow more diversified and heterogeneous. The stoning of adulteresses under one interpretation of radical Shia is obviously incompatible with democratic equality, but then so was the branding of adulteresses in Puritan Massachusetts and so are burning crosses and "Christian" Ku Klux Klan lynchings.

Religion, then, is always an issue for secular democratic states, and it will certainly remain a significant issue in places like Afghanistan and Iraq as they emerge from traditional tyrannies— the one theocratic, the other secular. But it is no absolute bar to democracy, nor is it an impossible impediment in the way of Muslims (or Christians or Jews or Hindus) as they move gradually toward free civil society and democratic government. Indeed (ironically), even as it worries about religion in the Muslim world, the American administration is currently attempting to overcome some of the artificial consequences of the separation of church and state in the United States by developing policies of social welfare rooted in "faith-based civic institutions." Religion is especially important (again, Tocqueville) in democratizing societies of the kind the United States was in the 1830s to help glue together a culture under stress from and at risk of coming apart as a consequence of the burdens of modern freedom. The healthy liberal society is one held together by common beliefs even as it makes room for plural opinions and conflicting ideologies. It does not make war on religion but makes way for religions.

If the United States wants to practice democratization as part of a preventive democracy strategy aimed at crippling terrorism in the setting of Islamic culture, then, it will have to proceed with greater patience than it has shown heretofore, and with an understanding that democracy's special virtues of tolerance and pluralism are intended not just to protect the state from religion but to protect religion from the state. Yet the liberal propensity to protect religion by separating it from the state sometimes turns into an inclination to treat it as private rather than public. This can trivialize religious beliefs and deny their essentially public character, and offer justification to societies still gripped by religion's fervor for distrusting liberalism. Liberals worry that religion will undermine their freedoms, but the religious wonder whether they themselves will be tolerated by those who call themselves free. Try to find on American commercial network television or in the cynical secularism of most Hollywood films a portrait of religion that is something other than condescending or ridiculing, a picture of belief that suggests ardor without fanaticism, or a study of transcendental faith that is not mocking. Cable offers Christian evangelical alternatives, but McWorld's pop culture portrays evangelism as faintly ridiculous in the same way that it makes President Bush's religious convictions grounds for suspicion. In America's distrust for religion elsewhere in the world it is hard to recognize a nation conceived in Protestantism's cradle or a people who even today attend religious services more than peoples in any European democracy. Franklin Roosevelt condemned the Nazis in strong religious terms, Jimmy Carter was an unabashed evangelical as president, and a half-dozen Cold War presidents saw in the Soviet Union's "godlessness" the worst of its sins. The Congress still opens its sessions with a prayer and presidents have forever closed their speeches with "God bless America," yet President Bush is distrusted by many critics because he is an earnest Methodist with a certain born-again fervor. Pluralism should strengthen respect for religious diversity rather than censor religious ardor.

To warn against a gross export of America's experience with religion as its unique political institutions and aggressive secular values is not to say that its democratic experience and history of democratic practices cannot be made useful to others, or that American guidance and material support cannot help build civic infrastructure. It is only to say that America will not be able to make other nations into democracies solely by dint of its own will. Trying to do so is likely to create an environment in which what appears to Americans as a struggle to spread democracy and rights around the world will appear to others as bullying arrogance—a thinly veiled rationale for securing an American empire. When the hand holding the Bill of Rights that reaches out in friendship is seen as nothing but a gloved twin of the naked fist with which American conquers rogue states, liberation becomes another word for Pax Americana.

President Bush evinced some appreciation for the dangers of hubris when in a riposte to Al Gore in the second 2000 presidential debate he declared: "Our nation stands alone right now in the world in terms of power. And that's why we've got to be humble and yet project strength in a way that promotes freedom . . . if we are an arrogant nation, they'll view us that way, but if we're a humble nation, they'll respect us." Perhaps this was a beneficial consequence of Bush's Christian convictions. The events of 9/11, which might have reinforced the call to humility, seem however to have eroded it. Deeply angered by the terrorist assault (which explains almost everything the president has done since), George Bush was awakened to the "moral mission of America." And though he understood well enough that if the war on terrorism came to be seen as a religious war, America could be perceived as a conqueror, and although he insisted he wanted America "to be viewed as the liberator," he seemed finally unable to resist high moralizing in that tone of self-righteousness which, perhaps more than America's policies themselves, has set America's friends and allies at odds with it.

The president found himself caught on the horns of a dilemma reflecting a quandary for the West *tout court*: he wanted to promote human rights, freedom, and democracy as part of America's moral mission. He also wanted people to know the rights-value system "cannot be compromised" since it represented "God-given values." This was paradoxically to preach an American gospel whose message was that "these aren't United States–created values. These are values of freedom and the human condition and mothers loving their children. What's very important as we articulate foreign policy through our diplomacy and military action is that it never look like we are creating—we are the author of these values."[17] The president seemed at once to evoke that humility about which he had spoken in the campaign ("these are not just *our* values") and the hubris that had driven his administration since 9/11 ("America's mission is to enforce these values on the world by war if necessary"). Members of an administration increasingly "hell-bent on war" in Iraq[18] confronting a United Nations increasingly leery of entering such a war bristled with hubris. Secretary of Defense Rumsfeld competed with right-wing journalists who had labeled the French "surrender monkeys" by writing off what he called "old Europe," hinting that Germany belonged in a coterie of uncooperative nations that included Libya and Cuba. In his instant bestseller supporting war, Robert Kagan explained that Europeans were "from Venus" with wan spirits and pusillanimous wills, while the United States was "from Mars," attuned to the real world of vio-

---

[17] Woodward, *Bush at War*, p. 131.

[18] "Hell-Bent on War" was how *Newsweek* titled its cover essay on Iraq in its February 17, 2003, issue.

lence and anarchy and ready to subdue it by manly war.[19] Pundit Morton Kondracke boasted, with that swaggering abandon that cable television requires of its regulars, that the United States was "the most powerful country in the world by far, and a lot of pip-squeak wannabes like France resent the hell out of it"[20] Preventive war, even when directed at appropriate terrorist targets, may then quite easily appear hubristic even to friends and allies of America. When advanced without humility, even the peaceful agenda of preventive democracy may appear arrogant. Because it is a giant, America must always worry that even its best deeds will be apprehended by others as self-serving if not downright perfidious. A century ago, when America first embarked on the course of empire in the West, there were already concerns about what William T. Stead called the "Americanization of the World."[21]

One path to humility can be opened by appreciating the priority of citizenship in building an indigenous democratic society. Free institutions help forge free men and women but only men and women who strive for and know something of freedom can forge free institutions. Jefferson assumed in the Declaration of Independence that men are born free, yet he established the University of Virginia because he knew that real freedom was acquired—a product of education, learning, experience, and empowerment. The American founders had a keen insight into the need to create citizens if the new constitution was to be more than a parchment parapet against tyranny. The Bill of Rights, Madison liked to say, was so

[19] Kagan, *Of Paradise and Power.*

[20] Cited by Joseph S. Nye Jr., *The Paradox of American Power: Why the World's Only Superpower Can't Go It Alone* (New York: Oxford University Press, 2002), p. 157.

[21] William T. Stead, *The Americanization of the World* (London: H. Markley, 1902).

much paper and could be secured only by competent and engaged citizens. John Adams in Massachusetts, no less than Thomas Jefferson in Virginia, had insisted that free schools for those who would be citizens were the indispensable condition for democracy's flourishing. Tocqueville spoke wisely of men who were born not free but in need of a long "apprenticeship of liberty"—what he called the "most arduous" of all apprenticeships. Democracy's greatest historical prophet, Jean-Jacques Rousseau, grasped the core significance of the citizen. To those who cried out for patriotism, he replied: "There can be no patriotism without liberty; no liberty without virtue; no virtue without citizens; create citizens and you will have everything you need; without them, you will have nothing but debased slaves, from the rulers of the state downwards."[22]

Rousseau surmised that citizens were created not born, which is why his writings on education (*Emile: or, On Education* and *Julie: or, The New Eloise*) bear so heavily on his understanding of democracy. Liberty, he noted in his essay "Considerations on the Government of Poland," is a food easy to eat but hard to digest. Liberating men from tyranny is one thing, helping them develop the capacity to exercise their autonomy is quite another. President Bush believed freeing Iraqis from the brutal tyranny of Saddam was tantamount to making them free citizens. But to be freed from autocracy is not the same thing as being free to rule one's self. Changing masters does not end servitude. Had President Bush consulted America's greatest democratic philosopher, John Dewey, he would have been reminded that the prudent practice of democracy rests

---

[22] Jean-Jacques Rousseau, *A Discourse on Political Economy*, in *Social Contract and Discourses*, Everyman Edition (London: J. M. Dent and Company, 1913), p. 251.

on a sound philosophy of education, and he might have ordered his troops in Baghdad to bar looters not only from the oil ministry but from the schools, museums, and libraries as well.

The lesson for national security policy is clear: an America wishing to secure itself from terror by forging a world of free nations needs to be at least as interested in smart citizens as it is in smart bombs. America's first instinct in spending dollars abroad has been to train soldiers rather than to train citizens. It costs far more to do the former, even though doing the latter pays off far better for democracy.

Even as the United States makes common cause with friendly military elites in Pakistan, Egypt, and Saudi Arabia, spending billions on weaponry and military training, Saudi Arabia is funding fundamentalist religious schools under the leadership of Wahhabi Islamic militants in countries like Pakistan and Bosnia, where there has been insufficient Western funding to help found indigenous (not American-style) state schools. In Bosnia, for example, "a lot of time and money has been wasted here on poorly coordinated projects," according to a local critic; meanwhile Saudi Arabia has spent over $500 million in Bosnia, much of it "to spread its rigid interpretation of Islam in a land where most Muslims are not conspicuously pious."[23] The Saudis know that controlling education is a far better way to determine the future than controlling the flow of weapons or the training of military elites. The Western neglect of education leaves a vacuum fundamentalists are ready to fill. The Wahhabi pedagogy of Islamic orthodoxy, gender inequality, theocracy, and hatred for infidels trains new generations of Muslims as

---

[23] The local Bosnian critic is Zarko Papic, and both quotes are from Daniel Simpson, "A Nation Unbuilt: Where Did All That Money in Bosnia Go?," *New York Times*, February 16, 2003, sec. 4, p. 12.

warriors for Jihad; what would it take to turn them into impassioned citizens for democracy? America has hardly begun to consider the delicate pedagogical balance needed if a Muslim society is to have schools that breed civic spirit without mandating secularism, that embody Islamic values without breeding religious intolerance. There are models to be explored in Turkey, Bangladesh, Mozambique, and Sri Lanka, where Islamic public education has evolved without an anti-Western or antimodern bias. The lesson of education is that preventive war, even when successful, can at best do no more than extirpate today's terrorists. Preventive democracy grounded in civic education addresses those who might become terrorists tomorrow.

To be sure, the United States does face difficult paradoxes in supporting education in other cultures. A necessary respect for diversity and a humility about American pedagogy demand that Americans remain as humble about exporting education as they need to be about exporting democracy. At the same time, they need to help nurture alternatives to doctrinaire and orthodox forms of education abroad that look more like dogmatic indoctrination than pedagogy. How can President Musharraf of Pakistan offer an alternative to the more than thirty thousand Wahhabi madrasahs operating on Pakistani soil without a budget for an effective public education system? Pakistani intelligence has been adept at arresting terrorists but ineffective in arresting the growth of terrorism. Surely America can both help provide a budget and offer the fruits of research without becoming a colonial schoolmaster imposing American-style standards on the Pakistani education system. Cooperation with UNESCO and global NGOs with an interest in education as well as consultation with comparative education specialists in America's own excellent graduate schools of education could augment legitimacy, minimize the idea that education means

Americanization, and provide greater sensitivity to local cultural and historical standards.[24]

Congress understandably likes to see the "made in America" brand on all humanitarian and economic aid, but anonymous contributions may serve America's long-term interests much more effectively. The United States may spend up to $100 billion on its Iraq intervention. Imagine what such a budget might do if applied worldwide to societies currently unable to educate their children. Why can the United States spend on a crisis basis hundreds of billions of dollars for wars whose long-term results are anything but certain and buck at spending 1 percent of that on education assistance that would make war far less unlikely in the next generation? Education builds a framework for democracy, but it also builds a framework for economic growth (technical knowledge and skills), public health (sanitation, birth control, a decline in sexually transmitted diseases), and cultural stability (cultural literacy, tolerance for diversity). Ignorance does not by itself produce terrorism, but it produces many of the pathologies that permit terrorism to grow—including poverty, unemployment, bigotry, resentment, hatred for "others," and a passion for vengeance. The conviction that books are more powerful

---

[24] The University of Maryland's College of Education has conducted research on comparative education of special relevance to Islamic societies. See Jo-Ann Amadeo et al., *Civic Knowledge and Engagement: An IEA Study of Upper Secondary Students in Sixteen Countries* (Amsterdam: The International Association for the Evaluation of Educational Achievement, 1999); and Judith Torney-Purta et al., *Citizenship and Education in Twenty-eight Countries: Civic Knowledge and Engagement at Age Fourteen* (Amsterdam: The International Association for the Evaluation of Educational Achievement, 2001). Also see the World Education Reports from UNESCO and *Education Sector Strategy* (Washington, D.C.: World Bank, 1999). For information on the monitoring of standards in America's Muslim schools, consult the Council on Islamic Education.

than bullets is democracy's leading premise. It should also be the first premise in preserving democracy from terrorism.

It is no secret in the United States that crime, disease, and social pathology are all closely correlated with the absence of schooling. School dropouts make up the overwhelming majority of the American prison population. Jailhouse schooling is by far the best way for inmates to minimize the chances of recidivism once they are released.[25] Throughout the population, a low level of educational attainment remains the best predictor there is of poverty, poor health, heightened mortality, having children out of wedlock, and nearly every other indicator of failure in society. As crime is propelled by ignorance at home, terrorism appears as the leading edge of the educational deficit abroad. Like revolutionaries, anarchists, and other violent vanguards, terrorists themselves are often educated (which accounts in part for their leadership role); some of them are even educated in the very societies they come to detest (exposure allows them to put flesh on the bones of their arguments about the corruption and moral depravity of their enemies); but even where their education is more than vocational and technical—their apocalyptic doctrines often have deep theological or philosophical roots—their elite campaigns of hate and vengeance depend on the marginalization, ignorance, and bigotry of a much larger mass population that has grown up without the benefits of any education at all.

Traditional military weaponry fails to match up with and is thus incommensurable with the forces terrorists can bring to bear on democracy. But the forces of democracy and civic education match up with them superbly. Cosmopolitan learning speaks to ignorance, blunting the force of prejudice and attenuating hatred's rage.

[25] For statistical corroboration of this claim and a study of how education diminishes recidivism, see James Gilligan, *Preventing Violence* (New York: Thames & Hudson, 2001).

Moreover, it is cheaper to encourage indigenous democratic growth through education than to impose it from the outside with guns or with dollars aimed at compelling a particular exogenous economic or political model.

Projecting military might evokes the old world of sovereign nations. Invoking the power of education responds to the new world of global interdependence. Preventive war's drawbacks derive from its reliance on obsolete notions of how power works in a vanishing world ruled by nation-states. Preventive democracy's attractions are associated with its recognition of a world of interdependence. Hence, preventive democracy is less inclined to offer a starving nation wheat than to help it learn to cultivate its own crops, less inclined to focus on extraction of natural resources than on diversifying the economy and creating jobs; it is anxious to avoid (as in the American social movement slogan) "doing for others what they can do for themselves"; it is more concerned to help a country look like a free version of itself than to look like America. This demands cooperation and reciprocity, rather than "you scratch my back, I'll scratch yours" bilateralism and paternalistic aid.

In the end, people can only secure democracy for themselves. Imposing it from the outside with the best of intentions is still a recipe for failure. At the same time, there cannot be democracy in one nation but not in its neighbor, in the north but not in the south. Interdependence means democracy must work for everyone or it may in time work for none. Nurturing democracy within nations cannot succeed unless democracy also governs relations among nations. If the social contract cannot be extended to the planetary sphere, its terms are unlikely to be able to secure liberty and safety within nations. The ultimate objective of preventive democracy is then neither McWorld nor AmericaWorld but "CivWorld"—a world of citizens for whom the social contract extended worldwide has become a survival covenant.

9

CivWorld

The independence of States can no longer be understood apart
from the concept of interdependence. All States are
interconnected both for better and for worse.
—*Pope John Paul II*[1]

> Terrorism is a multilateral problem. You can-
> not defeat it in one nation. You need interna-
> tional police work, teamwork, international
> harmonization of laws. . . . You act unilaterally
> . . . that's the one thing that will kill you in the
> war on terrorism.
>
> —*General Wesley Clark*[2]

The irony of terrorism is that it can use the conventional military hegemony of America to its own advantage because its
cadres are relatively immune to conventional weapons, because as
General Wesley Clark notes above, terrorism is a multilateral problem. Neither containment nor preventive war directed at states can
stop it. Preventive democracy stands a much better chance. For

---

[1] Address of His Holiness to the Diplomatic Corps, Rome, January 13, 2003.

[2] Cited in Michael Tomasky, "Meet Mr. Credibility," *American Prospect*, vol.
14, no. 3 (March 2003).

democracy undoes the conditions that allow terrorism to flourish—draining the swamp in which noxious mosquitoes breed, as the popular metaphor has it. Unlike counterstate preventive war, it addresses terrorism directly and cannot be twisted to terrorism's purposes. But when preventive war against Jihad is directed against alleged terrorist proxies such as Iraq, even a successful war has the appearance of a crusade mimicking Jihad's own violence and feeding the fires that inflame it. (Before America settled on the inflammatory title "Shock and Awe" for its war in Iraq, it toyed with the even more incendiary term *Crusade*.) The civilian deaths the United States euphemistically portrayed as collateral damage were likewise read in different terms elsewhere.

In fact, in the war in Iraq there was a text, dictated by the American government and embraced by a majority of (but by no means all) the American people, and a subtext in whose distinctive narrative many people around the world found another meaning. The American text, inflected by exceptionalism, was 9/11 and what Americans regarded as the unique damage done to them by heinous acts of terror. It justified the war as fair retribution as well as active prevention against Saddam Hussein, a twenty-first-century Hitler, whose threat to destroy the world with weapons of mass destruction was stopped cold by a brave American army leading a coalition of the willing, despite a recalcitrant and cowardly United Nations. The subtext spoke of an America that exaggerated its own sufferings while diminishing those of others; of a war of aggression by the United States in which an arrogant behemoth flattened a brave but hopelessly overmatched desert squirrel. In this subtext, stripping the two adversaries of their rationales and justifications, forgetting whether America fought for honor and revenge or oil and empire, whether Saddam was a despised tyrant or a beloved modern-day Saladin, the encounter between the two armies was finally a matter of the privileged killing the marginalized and the wealthy bombarding the impoverished. Reproduced on the screen, the war offered to everyone but self-absorbed Americans a pixel portrait of arrogant techno-soldiers, their humanity encased in Kevlar body armor, their senses enhanced by lasers and nightvision, their nervous systems protected by gas masks and chemical suits, running a modern military colossus at warp speed over ragtag bands of militiamen armed with weapons from another generation and tactics from another century, who nonetheless were occasionally able to surprise and distress those intent on shocking and awing them into oblivion. Despite the radical asymmetry in forces—(in the words of a surrendering Iraqi colonel: "We are not cowards, but what is the point? I've got a rifle from World War II. What can I do against American warplanes?"),[3] the people who were supposed to welcome the invading army with open arms failed to do so. The "no contest" hyperbole with which Americans boasted about their overwhelming military superiority was the same "cakewalk" hubris which, to others, suggested a self-aggrandizing exercise in bullyboy imperialism by Americans striving to live up to their own hype.[4]

This skeptical perspective was not much evident in the United States in the period of rallying round the flag, but given the degree to which politics is perception, the outsiders' subtext, right or wrong, suggested that the war on Iraq was unlikely to improve America's standing globally, let alone impair global terrorism's threat to the United States. Despite intelligence efforts and increased cooperation among national police and military intelli-

[3] Colonel Ahmed Ghobashi, cited by Dexter Filkins, "As Many Iraqis Give Up, Some Fight Fiercely," *New York Times*, March 23, 2003, p. B1.

[4] Ken Adelman, a former Reagan administration national security official, had written a piece for the *Washington Post* in early 2002 entitled "Cakewalk in Iraq" (February 13, 2002, p. A27).

gence services, in the period between the Afghanistan and Iraq operations there were deadly terrorist attacks against a synagogue in Djerba, Tunisia (April 2002), the Sheraton Hotel in Karachi (May 2002), the American Consulate in Karachi (June 2002), a nightclub in Bali (October 2002), and a hotel and an airplane in Kenya (November 2002), killing 236 people in total and wounding many more while spreading fear in the ubiquitous world of "soft targets." Following the war in Iraq, attacks were successfully carried out in Riyadh in Saudi Arabia and Casablanca in Morocco (both in May 2003). Thus does preventive war reinforce the image of America as a hubristic conqueror hiding behind a rhetoric of high moral purpose and democratic idealism without actually impacting terrorism.

Preventive democracy, on the other hand, addresses the subtext directly by working to turn the swamp where terrorism breeds into productive soil, by seeding it with all that it lacks—learning, liberty, self-government, opportunity, and security. It saps terrorism of its capacity to build on the alleged hypocrisy and hubris of its Western enemies. Because it empowers the powerless, genuine democracy offers precisely what those drawn by terrorism's self-destructive tactics lack: the capacity to control their own destinies. Tennyson imagined a "Parliament of Man" that would embody a cosmopolitan tolerance and empower self-governance. Terrorist jujitsu worked wonders with Western technology and weaponry, but it can do little to leverage such ideals as these to its own purposes. Liberty can no more be hijacked than equality can be simulated.

Democracy too has costs, of course, above all the time it takes and the patience it requires. As Joseph Nye observes, civil cooperation around the soft power of culture, civil society, and ideology—a useful specification of preventive democracy—can require "years of patient, unspectacular work, including close civilian cooperation with other countries."[5] Among those hungry for freedom, a call for patience can seem a self-serving caution by those who prefer not to help. But it actually mandates more deliberate, long-term and persistent engagement. Like a fickle teenager, attention-deficit America too often loses interest in previous conquests as soon as it acquires its latest. In 2002, the United States spent the largest share of its Afghan aid on humanitarian projects. But this year, according to *Washington Post* staff writer Marc Kaufman, despite the fact that "virtually every significant system in the country is broken," we will spend more on "building up the army, which has 3,000 members but is scheduled to reach 70,000." Aid has fallen from what the Bush administration initially projected to levels so low that Afghan finance minister Ashraf Ghani now fears "Afghanistan will become a narco-terrorist state that will be a constant problem to the world"—that is, if there still is an Afghan state when America finishes funding the "local militias and warlords that its military believes it needs in the war against Muslim extremists."[6] Involving civilians who can sustain cooperation rather than soldiers engaged in a perpetual standoff with invisible enemies, preventive democracy demands not only that countries work together but that civic association and nongovernmental organizations work together; and that individuals engage in citizen-to-citizen exchanges via both old and new technologies. Above all, it demands learning as a prerequisite of liberty. Afghanistan needs seventy thousand teachers. With them in place, it might not require seventy thousand soldiers.

Forging global democracy among nations is little less difficult than forging democracy within nations emerging from traditional-

[5] Nye, *The Paradox of American Power*, p. xv.

[6] Marc Kaufman, "Embracing Nation-Building," *Washington Post National Weekly Edition*, April 21–27, 2003, p. 16.

ism, tyranny, or war. In the traditional state-to-state interactions that led to the "concert of nations" approach to international relations, citizens were at best represented by their governments, and at worst merely stood by as their passive subjects. In the new forms of citizen-to-citizen interaction called for by preventive democracy, citizens and their civic associations represent themselves, seeking global forms of democratic governance founded on civic and third sector cooperation. The aim cannot initially be global democratic governance on the model of "world federalism" or "world government," but is rather a more modest laying of foundations for global civic cooperation—the achievement of a "CivWorld" that is civic, civil, and civilized and hence nurturing to transnational forms of citizenship. This is no easy task and requires more than rhetorical appeals. Although Europe has learned to pool sovereignty and abjure traditional models of sovereign independence, it has still not achieved a robust sense of regional citizenship. The euro remains today a more convincing symbol of regional identity than the European.

Citizenship has always been attached to activities and attitudes associated with the neighborhood ("Liberty is municipal!" was Alexis de Tocqueville's greatest insight): this means that imagining what global citizenship actually entails is a daunting task. Still, it is absolutely necessary, because while participation is local, power is global: unless local citizens can become globally engaged, the true levers of power will remain beyond their grasp.

A hint of what transnational citizenship can accomplish is evident in the emerging voice of global public opinion. Hardly audible a generation ago, the spontaneous collective voice of citizens today can be heard speaking to issues that go far beyond their neighborhoods—suggesting that interdependence makes the idea of a global neighborhood less of an oxymoron than it used to be. When the aging former Chilean dictator General Augusto Pinochet was arrested in England in October 1998 on a Spanish warrant requesting his extradition on murder charges, first the House of Lords and then foreign minister Jack Straw ruled that the arrest and extradition bid were legal: but the impetus for the actions was not a Spanish vendetta or an English commitment to the rule of law but global indignation. Although Pinochet's failing health ultimately led to his release and return to Chile two years later, "retired" dictators will never again feel safe from the power of international public opinion.[7]

Similarly, when an international campaign to ban land mines (ICBL) eventuated in a 1997 treaty (the Ottawa Convention) that today has secured nearly 140 signatories (though not the signature of the United States), the sponsors were not leading governments but a New England activist named Jody Williams and her many citizen partners (including land mine victims, Princess Diana, and a number of engaged NGOs such as Human Rights Watch and Physicians for Human Rights) worldwide. Williams won the 1997 Nobel Peace Prize for her remarkable work, but the real victor was, Williams herself insisted, the newly empowered voice of global opinion. "It wasn't until the voice of civil society was raised to such a high degree that governments began to listen, that change began to move the world, with lightning and unexpected speed," Williams told the delegates assembled in Canada to sign the treaty.[8]

---

[7] Ironically, this has made it somewhat more difficult to talk sitting dictators into exile (as in the case of Saddam Hussein), because an agreement by governments that they will not be prosecuted can no longer be counted on in the face of global public opinion. Even Henry Kissinger risks trial on charges stemming from alleged activities in Cambodia during the war in Vietnam if he travels to France or certain other countries where an indictment has been threatened. See Christopher Hitchens, *The Trial of Henry Kissinger* (New York: Verso, 2001) and the film of the same name by Eugene Jarecki.

[8] Jody Williams, address to the Treaty Signing Convention, Ottawa, Canada, December 3, 1997. For updates on this work, see the annual Landmine Monitor Reports published by Human Rights Watch.

Global public opinion has taken to the streets in recent years, making its voice felt as well as heard. In the so-called antiglobal-ization movement, which is better understood as a "democratize globalization" movement, international groups like ATTAC (orig-inally founded by the McDonald's tormentor, French farmer José Bové) and a host of older NGOs captured the attention first of the media and then of international financial institutions such as the World Bank, the International Monetary Fund, and the World Trade Organization (the "IFIs"). Their protest activities at key global meetings in Seattle, Prague, Washington, Rome, and Davos have forced governments to look more critically at the impact of banks, speculative capital, and international trade treaties on marginalized peoples who were previously voiceless in the world's power councils. These same activists have also pro-duced an annual "counter-Davos" (as an alternative to the World Economic Forum at Davos) convening in Porto Allegre, Brazil, which has helped focus research, scholarship, and public opinion on issues of global economic development. Indeed, it has forced the corporate forum at Davos to consider the interests of civil society and the NGOs and not focus exclusively on the interests of global capital.

Spontaneous protest movements guided by the World Wide Web and a host of otherwise distinctive NGOs have also had a pro-found impact on the debate over the American decision to invade Iraq without United Nations approval, not by preventing war but by making manifest the widespread international opposition to American unilateralism and its reliance on purely military and pre-ventive war solutions. A group called MoveOn helped coordinate the coalition of groups (including True Majority and Win Without War) that facilitated demonstrations by hundreds of thousands of Americans who felt unrepresented in the tepid conversations held about the war in Congress before its onset or by the pusillanimous caution of "opposition party" politicians both before and during the war.[9] Their Democracy in Action movement continued to embody the vitality and relevance of global public opinion all the way through the war and into the period of anarchy known as "reconstruction."

Popular culture's representatives in Nashville and Hollywood have played a more controversial role in moving public opinion. The views of musicians and actors can be as uninformed and demagogic as radio's infamous talk show hosts, but some artists who combine thoughtfulness, dedication, and action have had a significant impact on governments as well as on public opinion. Adam Yauch and Adam Horowitz of the Beastie Boys have campaigned with discipline and without demogoguery on behalf of a free Tibet, while the pop singer Bono turned a personal commitment to publicizing the AIDS crisis in Africa into an official U.S. government program by persuading then treasury secretary Paul O'Neill to accompany him in 2002 on an African AIDS safari that produced real changes in the Bush administration's policy toward the HIV crisis (including significantly increased funding). Singing groups such as the Dixie Chicks and others too closely associated with perpetual liberal protest have been tracked by the traditional right and denied radio airplay by stations that may or may not be acting in collusion with partisan ideologues, but on the whole the engagement of popular artists in civic protest has helped spark expression on the part of many people otherwise left mute in the debates over war and peace.[10]

[9] There were a few exceptions, including Senator Robert C. Byrd of West Virginia, who spoke fervently in opposition to war, but most Americans wishing to hear a strong and ongoing debate were left feeling voiceless.

[10] Despite complaints about leftist celebrities, as Warren St. John notes, "while politically active stars have long provoked strong reactions from those who disagree with them—think of Jane Fonda, Edward Asner and Charlton Heston—opposition to celebrity activities has never been more vocal or better

Preventive democracy begins with citizens and the expression of civic views, but has extended its compass to activities that move beyond protest against (or support for) official government policies. MoveOn offered a Citizens' Declaration that read simply: "As a US-led invasion of Iraq begins, we, the undersigned citizens of many countries, reaffirm our commitment to addressing international conflicts through the rule of law and the United Nations."[11] There are other examples, such as an affirmation that captures the reality of interdependence and takes the form of a Declaration of Interdependence. This CivWorld manifesto and others like it hope to stand to the coming age as the American Declaration of Independence stood to America's founding era. Jefferson's Declaration embodied the principles of Hobbes and Locke at the level of a nation, a people bound together and submitting to law because they understood that liberty is more secure under the law than under the rule of the strong, that safety cannot be assured by anarchy in the state of nature. But in creating a world of independent sovereign peoples, the logic of nation-states issued in a new anarchy, a fearful Hobbesian state of nature among nations. The new Declaration of Interdependence takes the logic of covenant to the global level, thus:

---

organized. Web sites with names like boycott-hollywood.net, Famousidiot.com, and Celiberal.com are spearheading email and telephone campaigns against stars and, in the case of television performers, the companies that advertise on their shows" ("The Backlash Grows Against Celebrity Activists," *New York Times*, March 23, 2003, sec. 9, p. 1, 2003). Paul Krugman has speculated about the role of radio behemoths like Clear Channel that have "close links to the Bush administration." See "Channels of Influence," *New York Times*, March 25, 2003, 2003, p. A17.

[11] See the MoveOn Web site at www.moveon.org.

DECLARATION OF INTERDEPENDENCE

We the people of the world do herewith declare our interdependence both as individuals and legal persons and as peoples—members of distinct communities and nations. We do
pledge ourselves citizens of one CivWorld, civic, civil, and civilized. Without prejudice to the goods and interests of our
national and regional identities, we recognize our responsibilities to the common goods and liberties of humankind as a
whole.

   We do therefore pledge to work both directly and through
the nations and communities of which we are also citizens:

- To guarantee justice and equality for all by establishing on a
  firm basis the human rights of every person on the planet,
  ensuring that the least among us may enjoy the same liberties as the prominent and the powerful;
- To forge a safe and sustainable global environment for all—
  which is the condition of human survival—at a cost to peoples based on their current share in the world's wealth;
- To offer children, our common human future, special attention and protection in distributing our common goods, above
  all those upon which health and education depend;
- To establish democratic forms of global civil and legal governance through which our common rights can be secured and
  our common ends realized;
  and
- To foster democratic policies and institutions expressing and
  protecting our human commonality;
  and still at the same time,
- To nurture free spaces in which our distinctive religious, ethnic, and cultural identities may flourish and our equally worthy lives may be lived in dignity, protected from political,
  economic, and cultural hegemony of every kind.

This particular declaration—one can imagine many others—has the advantage of existing in a practical citizens campaign that offers a program for global civil society and democracy.[12] There are many other organizations and associations within and among nations, nongovernmental organizations and civil society institutions, that share the goal of a planet on which peace and liberty are the offspring of law and cooperation rather than war and unilateralism. Some are rights groups like Human Rights Watch or corruption monitors like Transparency International; some are movements like the one offering poor women microcredit initiated by the Bangladesh Grameen Bank and extended by the Bangladesh Rural Advancement Committee (BRAC),[13] and international boycott organizations like Dolphin-Safe Tuna and Rugmark; others are umbrella groups such as Civicus, that act as nerve centers for other NGOs; still others, despite specialized aims, have become "generic" NGOs, like Doctors Without Border (Médecins Sans Frontières, winner of the 1999 Nobel Peace Prize) and Amnesty International, and have come to stand for the possibility of collaboration across frontiers.

A list is not the same thing as a global civil society, but when it

---

[12] The CivWorld Global Citizens Campaign, whose activities include a signature campaign for the Declaration of Interdependence; an annual Interdependence Day to be celebrated for the first time in Philadelphia and a number of world capitals, as well as college and school campuses, on September 12, 2003; a global citizenship education curriculum for adults and schools; a global citizens passport; and art and music activities recognizing the arts as a natural commons for the human spirit. See the Web site www.civworld.org.

[13] Bangladesh is a laboratory of civic innovation, with over twenty thousand NGOs registered with the government. BRAC runs thousands of health clinics and oversees thirty-four thousand schools with more than a million students, and with its business and microcredit banking ventures, which rival the Grameen Bank, it "may be the world's largest national nongovernmental organization." See Amy Waldman, "Helping Hand for Bangladesh's Poor," *New York Times*, March 25, 2003, p. A8.

encompasses not dozens or hundreds but thousands of transnational civic associations, a start has been made. Led by citizens rather than by governments, the organizations focus civic power on intractable political problems that recalcitrant governments are not addressing. They are not democratically constituted (neither transparent nor accountable), but in their plurality and diversity they embody the richness of civil society. They lack formal power and the capacity to enforce their prudent ideas, however, and so have not deflected global markets from their predatory practices or impeded the course of America's fear-driven preventive war strategy or insulated the world's children from the ravages of crime, land mines, and AIDS—and are unlikely to anytime soon, unless they can join forces with formal governments and transnational political institutions.

Yet in a world where there are diseases as well as doctors without frontiers, corruption and prostitution as well as Interpol cops without frontiers, and terrorists and wars against terrorists as well as peacemaking NGOs without frontiers, the time has surely come for citizens without frontiers. Without them, lex humana will remain a dream and such formal international governance institutions as can be contrived will be without substance or effect. Without them, global education, global cooperation, global law, and global democracy are empty phrases. The paradox is that global citizens are most likely to be produced by the global education, global cooperation, global law, and global democracy that global citizens produce.

Throughout the period prior to the Iraq invasion, the argument turned on whether it was President Bush or President Hussein who held the keys to war and peace. Oddly, the man who said he would end the war others started at a time and place of his choosing declared right up to the day American forces deployed for action in Iraq that it was actually all up to Saddam Hussein. Disarm, and he could save his skin, his country, and the peace. In truth, as far as democracy is concerned, what happened yesterday in Iraq and what may happen tomorrow in North Korea, Iran, Syria, Yemen, Indonesia, Pakistan, and the Philippines depends neither on an American commander in chief presiding over Pax Americana nor on adversarial government leaders trying to impede the progress of America's fear-driven imperium.

Democratic outcomes depend on democratic struggle and the readiness of citizens—or those who would be citizens—to wage it. This is the core meaning of citizenship. Noisy dissidents like Abou Jahjah in Belgium or Michael Moore in the United States (who disrupted the 2003 Academy Awards by waving his Oscar and ranting theatrically about a "fictitious war" and a "fictitious president") are not betrayers of democracy; they are civic alternatives to fear. When they are silenced, fear succeeds, and the victory of fear is the triumph of terrorism even if terrorist cells are broken and terrorist agents destroyed, even if the nations that harbor and support them are subjected to the awesome power of the American colossus and collapse. When citizens fail, imperious leaders are able to match fear for fear with their adversaries, and all too quickly there are no citizens—only masters and their subjects. At the height of the American campaign against Baghdad, civic dissent in America seemed to many to have been put on hold. Criticizing the president who had put American troops in harm's way on the basis of palpable deceptions and blatant lies somehow was equated with betraying the troops the president put in harm's way. Preventive war was doing a better job at preventing democracy than preventing terror.

Fighting terrorism with preventive democracy also risks hubris. Exceptionalism has always spoken in democracy's name and has today become one of preventive war's leading rationales. Perhaps, skeptics will conclude, preventive democracy is only imperialism's newest disguise. It can be but it need not be. America is unique

among nations today not because it is different but because it is so
much like the world. A multicultural nation whose majority will
soon comprise a host of minorities and whose society looks more
and more like the world it paradoxically refuses to join can, if it
wishes, promote its diversity as a model for others; a society of
global cities is well suited to global democratic leadership; tolerance, humility, inventiveness and a belief in self-government as a
product of local ingenuity are values that others can emulate without feeling like they are being colonized. President Bush's wisest
words were the ones he spoke when he told Americans that rights
are given to humankind by God and belong to no nation or government. Kofi Annan tried to respond to American critics of the
United Nations by reminding them that "the United Nations is not
a separate or alien entity, seeking to impose its agenda on others.
The United Nations is us: it is you and me."[14] In this same sense,
the United States *is* the United Nations: America *is* the world and
need not conquer it in order to join it.

[14] Kofi Annan, speech at College of William and Mary, Williamsburg, Va., February 8, 2003; cited in Julia Preston, "Annan Appeals to U.S. for More Talks
Before the War," *New York Times*, February 9, 2003, sec. 1, p. 15.

Conclusion

Before it establishes its worldly dominion, fear's empire colonizes the imagination. War is a necessary but poor instrument against terror even when focused exclusively on actual perpetrators. It inspires fear in all who engage in it. But soldiers at least are active: in democratic wars they are citizens-at-arms who can subdue their own fear through engagement. Action is the cloak in which courage wraps itself. The least frightened if most put-upon people in the days following that unluckiest of mornings on September 11, 2001, were those called to Ground Zero, first to search for survivors, then to rescue from oblivion and afford human remains some minimal dignity, and finally to clear the rubble while sanctifying the site. Because they were doers not watchers, because their actions allowed them to engage terrorism by addressing its consequences, at least while they were at work, they were immunized to some degree against the fears and anxieties afflicting the rest of America.[1] To be a New Yorker in those days was perhaps to feel slightly more active, engaged, affected, and hence slightly less helpless than other Americans—though New Yorkers and those from the local tri-state region were the "victims" of the attack and presumably especially likely targets of any subsequent attack that

---

[1] The Pentagon was also a target, but there soldiers and soldier civilians were at work, and the dynamics (though not the tragedy and the impact of the losses) were a little different.

might be launched. When the passengers on the last terrorist flight being diverted to Washington rushed the cabin to forestall still another catastrophe, even as they went to certain deaths, they transformed themselves from victims into actors, from subjects into citizens. A better way to die and surely a better way to live.

The empire of fear is a realm without citizens, a domain of spectators, of subjects and victims whose passivity means helplessness and whose helplessness defines and sharpens fear. Citizenship builds walls of activity around fear: this cannot prevent the doing of terrorist deeds, but it diminishes the psychic toll that terrorism takes. President Bush squandered a unique opportunity following 9/11 when the nation cried out for engagement and the president, understandably anxious to restore a sense of normalcy to a rattled people, urged them to go shopping.[2] Where citizens yearned to be responders, their government asked them to be consumers. Where spectators wished to become involved agents, their deputies insisted it wasn't necessary. It *was* necessary. To relinquish fear people must step out of paralysis. The president suggested they step into the mall.

With the approach of war in Iraq, the mistake was repeated. Only opponents of the war had the chance to actively express their dissent. The majority remained bystanders and spectators, women and men uncertain of the cause but willing to be engaged—without a theater in which to play out their civic sentiments, however, other than to wave flags and anxiously watch. They hoped to participate in war's sacrifices but were told not to worry. They longed as people to share in its costs and were offered a tax reduction. Some might have wished they had been called to serve, but Amer-

---

[2] The missed opportunity was the more surprising coming from a president who, though generally wed to the ABC (anything but Clinton) approach to his agenda, had embraced Clinton's national service programs at the Corporation for National and Community Service.

ica's army is now a cadre of technical professionals schooled in an advanced weaponry that makes the citizen-soldier obsolete. (Other than in the officer corps, it also draws from those in need of opportunity and is thus not quite as "voluntary" as it claims.) Secretary of Defense Rumsfeld spoke dismissively of conscripts in the new "army of one" peopled exclusively by professionals. Yet the rationale for citizens serving in war is grounded in democracy itself and cannot be dismissed by technical considerations. War is always democracy's last resort, and it is in order to keep it that way that citizens are asked to make the ultimate sacrifice in common. Without a conscript army, America might still be in Vietnam. With only a single member of Congress with a child serving in the military, congressional support for war unending had become frighteningly unproblematic by the onset of war. Congressman Charles B. Rangel of New York stirred the pot by calling for the reintroduction of conscription in autumn of 2002, but his appeal was written off as mere politics, an antiwar ploy. Yet though they may be inconvenient in an age of smart weapons and professional wars, citizen-soldiers are at the heart of the democratic project and a crucial way to unite a strategy of counterterrorist preventive war with a strategy of preventive democracy.

Moderns caught up in the imperatives of interdependence have but two options: to overpower the malevolent interdependence that is terrorism by somehow imposing a global pax rooted in force; or to forge a benevolent interdependence by democratizing the world. Other nations cannot pursue preventive democracy in the absence of American participation or in the presence of American hostility. Is America up to the challenge? Hard to know.

If Americans cannot find their way out of fear's realm, they are lost. No friendly European ally will dissuade them from the course of war, no adversarial rogue state will seem puny enough to ignore. Since fear is about perception not reality, the terrorists can win without firing a shot. They need only stoke the American imagination—or stoke the imagination of those in government and the media entrusted with stoking the public's imagination. Nine-eleven was a horrendous day that exacted a terrible price from individual American families, and (we are promised) there will be others. But as an assault on America's powerful common body, such attacks are as bee stings to a grizzly bear, momentary flashes of pain easily brushed off with the swipe of America's massive paws. America cannot at once be as powerful as it boasts and as vulnerable as it fears. Its power belies its fear—or should. This is not to minimize the personal tragedy visited on terror's victims or argue that the war against terrorism should not be fought. It is only to maintain a perspective that remembers terrorism is a function of powerlessness and hurts the powerful only as they allow themselves to be hurt. Democracy defeats terrorism because democracy makes imagination into a tool of empathy and action, depriving it of the anxieties that beset it when it is otherwise idle or taken in by fear's grim games.

There is a tendency to treat claims about democracy's virtues as romantic or idealistic or even utopian. Perhaps they are. Civilization itself, Yeats wrote, is hooped together by a web of illusion, and democracy is surely among the most seductive of such illusions. But in this new era of interdependence where criminals and terrorists know that power resides not with sovereign nations but in the interstices between them, democracy has become a counsel of realists. The "Star Spangled Banner," penned by Francis Scott Key watching the British bombardment of Baltimore in 1814, was long the martial anthem of a sovereign and independent United States. "America the Beautiful," written by the poet Katharine Lee Bates as she gazed up at the front range of the soaring Rockies in 1893, speaks to an America today impelled to embrace the world out of necessity. Bates, a practiced critic of America's first age of imperialism at the end of the nineteenth century, knew the secret of liberty's preservation:

> *America! America!*
> *God mend thine every flaw,*
> *Confirm thy soul in self-control,*
> *Thy liberty in law.*

In the more prosaic words of social science realism, "a rule-based international order, especially one in which the U.S. uses its political weight to derive congenial rules, will most fully protect American interests, conserve its power, and extend is influence."[3] Such rules must apply to all. President Dwight Eisenhower cautioned Americans to recognize that "there can be no peace without law. And there can be no law if we were to invoke one code of international conduct for those who oppose us, and another for our friends."[4]

The romantic idealists today are the eagles, clinging to the hope that America's ancient prerogatives and classical sovereignty embodied in the will to war are enough to overcome interdependence. Realists—often military men like Eisenhower was—have become owls, yielding to interdependence and seeking to enact preventive democracy both as a short-term prophylactic against terrorism and a long-term strategy aimed at educating citizens and placing them at the center of national and global life. Realist logic treats power and fear as antonyms. Real power today lies in being

---

[3] Ikenberry, "American Imperial Ambition."

[4] President Dwight Eisenhower, presidential radio address, October 31, 1956.

able to will common global laws rather than in asserting individual national sovereignty. The logic of liberty and the logic of security can be joined: their buckle is democracy. Over true democracy, over the women and men whose engaged citizenship constitutes true democracy, fear's empire holds no sway.

Index